Backroads

Blessings from the Blue Ridge —
Lynn Coffey

Backroads

Plain Folk and Simple Livin'

Lynn Coffey

Quarter Books

Cover design by Jane Hagaman
Cover art by Lynn Coffey, View of the Tye River Valley from 20-Minute Cliff
    (Milepost 19 on the Blue Ridge Parkway)
Author photograph by Bob Nelms
Interior design by Jane Hagaman
Unless noted, all interior photos by Lynn Coffey

Page 96: "Water Lily Nymphaea Foxfire" © by Hayden Bird/iStockphoto
Page 135: "Autumn on Blue Ridge Parkway" © by Dave Hughes/iStockphoto

Quartet Books
PO Box 4204
Charlottesville, VA 22905

If you are unable to order this book from your local
bookseller, you may order directly from the author.
Call 540-949-0329 or use the order form in the back
of the book.

ISBN 978-0-615-31223-1

10 9 8 7 6 5 4 3 2 1

Printed on acid-free paper in the United Sates

Florence Gains (Meade)
Lynchburg 434-929-2688

Sec @ Oak Hill Church Library
Pamela Turner
cell 518-339-9216

SCORE

WE	THEY	WE	THEY	WE	THEY

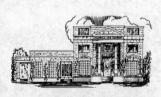

Dedicated to the mountain people:
who taught me everything I value and hold dear

Forest and Eve Coffey, Love, Virginia

Contents

Foreword

I first met Lynn Coffey more than a dozen years ago while I was immersed in a search for virtue in America. My wife Amy and I had embarked on a ten-month cross-country excursion to research a book I had conceived called *States of Mind*. Ours was a figurative search. Can we find honor? Pride? Faith? Wisdom? But we made it a literal one by visiting hamlets well off the beaten path. So we explored Honor, Michigan . . . and Pride, Alabama . . . and Faith, South Dakota . . . and Wisdom, Montana. We wondered: Would we be able to find paragons of such virtues in the overlooked and underappreciated nooks and crannies of the country?

That's how we found our way to the Blue Ridge Parkway in Virginia and to a turnoff at Milepost 16 that led to a tiny hamlet called Love.

At the Nelson County Visitor Center, a kindly gentleman pointed us to page 60 of *What to Do and See in the Shenandoah Valley* and a small boxed advertisement for *Backroads*, which was described as a "homespun newsletter about backroad ramblin', plain folks and simple living." For more information, readers were advised to contact Lynn Coffey. There were only eighty-five people in Love, so she wasn't hard to find.

When we arrived at the two-story log home that Lynn and her husband Billy had built themselves, the one with the gentle creek meandering through the front yard and the wide front porch with a bench swing offering a view of the George Washington National

Forest . . . I thought, *simple living.* We sat with the Coffeys at a long kitchen table handmade by the two of them, surrounded by artifacts that would have seemed anachronistic nearly anywhere else but there—a wood-burning stove, a pie safe, an old Victrola. And I thought, *plain folks.*

Naturally, I liked them immediately. I must assume everyone does. Billy is hard-working and soft-spoken and kind. Lynn is sweet and curious and eminently hospitable. Coffee may be an acquired taste (I have yet to acquire it), but it is impossible to dislike the Coffeys.

On the wall of the kitchen, there was a plaque with a heart burned into it and the words, *Love, VA . . . Billy + Lynn . . . November 23, 1992.* The story behind that well describes the contents of this book.

You see, Lynn had a neighbor who was unable to reach her house due to a fallen tree. Billy, born and raised in a bare-bones cabin in nearby Chicken Hollow, worked the night shift at the time, so he was available to assist. Billy and Lynn had known each other for more than a decade, had attended the same church at the top of the mountain, and had watched the children from their first marriages grow up together. So she called him, and he took a chainsaw to the tree. And Lynn wound up riding home with him that day. "That's when it started," she told me. They were married the following year.

So yes, these two residents of Love are very much in love. But the other part of the story is this: Love thy neighbor. And that's what *Backroads* is all about.

Lynn had been born into a family of "city folk" in Florida, but had always yearned for unadorned simplicity. She found it in on Meadow Mountain, a place where your family tends to be your neighbors and your neighbors tend to become family. She realized, too, that the mountain culture that so appealed to her was ever so slowly ebbing toward oblivion. Somebody had to chronicle its wonders before it was gone. "I just thought their lives were worth recording," said Lynn. "So I just started to talk to everybody."

That's why it is somewhat ironic for me to write something called a foreword. Because, in many ways, *Backroads* is a look back—a window into the past. The first issue appeared in December 1981. It was a little rural newspaper dedicated to "the small mountain hamlets that dot the American landscape and to the special people who inhabit them." That summer made me realize that Lynn was doing exactly what I was doing on my grand book-research tour, only on a more intimate scale.

My theory is this: The metaphors that we have long used to describe America are rather inadequate. I never quite bought into the notion that we could call ourselves a melting pot or a patch-work quilt. To me, America is a masterpiece of pointillism—a dot painting. And by dots, I mean the smallest ones on the map. The colors blend together from a distance, but they stand out boldly when inspected more closely. To truly understand America, I believe that you have to connect the dots.

So Lynn Coffey began to celebrate those dots—the ones so small that they couldn't even be found on most maps. Here was a simple woman (in the most admirable sense) producing a paean to the simple life. Leave the stress-inducing headlines to the big-city journalists. Lynn's stories announced things like "How the Mason Jar Got Its Name." And "Making Hand Cranked Ice Cream." And "Whatever Happened to String?" When Love finally received private phone lines in 1986, Lynn ran the story under the headline: "Death of the Party Line."

She paid for printing costs with income from local advertisers, who received a stack of copies to hand out at their places of business. When locals started asking for extra copies for cousins and friends, the circulation grew, as did the size of the monthly newsletter. By the time I arrived in May 1996, *Backroads* was a twenty-four-page publication with nearly a thousand subscribers in more than two-dozen states. "But they're still free if you want 'em," Lynn insisted. People told her she could benefit by charging, say, a dollar apiece. But she would have none of it. Her philosophy: Where else can you get free good news?

But it wasn't really news. You want that? Turn to the *Washington Post*. You want insight into a community, a culture, a way of life? Turn to Lynn Coffey.

She had just published the 172nd edition of *Backroads* when I came into her life. She would go on to continue the labor of love for another decade. Her little hobby became a mission of sorts—and a treasure trove of mountain lore, mountain humor, mountain history, and, most of all, mountain people. Whenever a family held a reunion or a pig roast, Lynn was there with a pen (the writing kind) and a smile. In fact, I would think there may be nobody on Meadow Mountain that she doesn't know.

The regular features in Backroads included a "Love Notes" section ("Get well wishes to Gene Everitt, who was in the hospital last month."), and "Helpful Hints" ("When making blackberry pie, sprinkle the bottom crust with cracker crumbs so the juice won't ooze out."). There were regular columns with names like "Down at the Store" and "Old Truck Corner." And there was a "What Is It?" section, which presented a photo of an obscure implement (say, a welder's chipping hammer or a grapefruit corer) and then revealed the item's identity the following month.

This book that you hold in your hands is a sort of Greatest Hits of *Backroads*, although there is fodder for a great many more books after this. And the whole is greater than the sum of the parts. When you read about butchering hogs or rendering lard or spring sheep shearing, you're gaining an understanding of the blood, sweat, and tears of Appalachian survival. When you read about people like Oscar Randolph Fitch and Ethna Fauber Seaman, you're being transported through the generations. When you drool at the mountain recipes (Nin's Homemade Hoecake!) and grin at the mountain superstitions (Picking up a spoon found by the side of the road is bad luck!) and raise an eyebrow at the mountain cures (Smearing the head with cow manure cures baldness!), you are gradually becoming part of that very mountain yourself.

"She can take nothing and make a story out of it. She really can," Billy declared to me as we sat around that kitchen table many years ago. It seemed to me that he assumed a city slicker like myself would think his wife's newsletter was indeed making something out of nothing. But I knew better. *Backroads* preserves a slowly dwindling culture. For the people in the hollows of the Blue Ridge, it isn't nothing. It is a compendium of everything.

Brad Herzog
September 2009

Acknowledgments

No book is written entirely by one individual. It is the combined effort of those who caught the vision the author intended and saw it to fruition. So it is with gratitude that I thank each person who played a part in the completion of *Backroads: Plain Folk and Simple Livin'*.

Rick Williams, longtime friend and author of three books about the Civil War era, who encouraged me from the beginning with his "you can do it" attitude. Rick was always more than willing to answer any of my questions and share what he knew about the publishing business.

Brad and Amy Herzog, who immortalized Billy and me in Brad's 1999 book, *States of Mind*, and ten years later honored me by writing the foreword in my own book. Although distance separates us, you'll always be friends and kindred spirits.

My publishing team at Quartet Books, who guided me through the entire process and believed the book had merit. Publicity agent Sara Sgarlat and her husband Leonard Baker, content editor, who were encouraging right from the start. Jane Hagaman, the cover design and page layout wizard who gave *Backroads* its beautiful form. Tania Seymour, who did the copyediting of the manuscript. Cynthia Mitchell, who did the proofreading and was responsible for finding the best prices for printing.

My patient husband Billy, who not only stood by me throughout this book project but for many years trooped around with me to interviews and family reunions and helped me deliver the *Backroads* newspaper—all without a single complaint. I could never have done what I did without his computer knowledge (of which I have none) and constant support.

My God, in awe and appreciation, who not only blessed me with the gift of writing but also arranged the symphony of my days that I might live the simple life I've always dreamed of and use my talent to bless others.

Introduction

As a small child, I was endlessly fascinated with thoughts of building a log cabin in the mountains and living a simplistic lifestyle. I was so young, in fact, that a good man never figured into the equation. How I hoped to accomplish this fantasy single-handedly was anybody's guess, but, then, dreams aren't so much about logic as they are imagination. It was one of those "take a trip without ever leaving the farm" types of things. The only problem was the *lack* of farm, since city parents in southern Florida were raising me. Passions of the heart are not easily snuffed out, however, and growing up, I found creative ways to fuel my dream.

Behind our house, there was an undeveloped wood that I constantly played in, making outlines of cabin interiors from fallen tree branches and bits of moss. By the time the woods succumbed to urban sprawl, I was enrolled in a high school agriculture class, which had a twenty-acre farm just west of town. For me, the farm was heaven on earth, and being the only female in a large class of rural boys, I soaked up information like a dry sponge. While other girls my age were going to dances and shopping for prom dresses, I was learning the fine art of stretching fences and raising hogs. Each learned skill was carefully tucked away in the part of me that instinctively knew that one day I'd be living my childhood dream.

Fast forward five years—I found myself married and living in Richmond, Virginia. Our family made the first trip to the Blue Ridge Mountains in January 1971, when my only daughter was five

months old. It became immediately apparent there was something
drawing me to the little hamlet of Love, Virginia, where we had
gone to visit friends of our Richmond neighbors. The village itself
was perched on top of a piece of land the locals called "Meadow
Mountain," which paralleled the Blue Ridge Parkway at milepost
16. Its perimeters wound down the mountain for about three miles
and included a parcel across the Parkway known as "Chicken
Holler." In 1976, we bought an acre of land where we planned to
build a house, and four years later, in the summer of 1980, we made
a permanent move to the mountains.

We rented, for the unbelievable price of one hundred dollars a
month, a rustic hunting camp that adjoined our property, and I
felt like Thoreau living on Walden Pond. The camp was old and
drafty, without a single bit of insulation stuffed in its cracks. Our
only heat source was a cast-iron wood stove located in the front of
the cabin, which had to be stoked full, dampers wide open, just to
take the chill off. With no ceiling, the heat went straight up . . .
and out. In the kitchen, the water in the cat's bowl froze into a
solid orb if we didn't empty it before bedtime. Even with the lack
of modern amenities, I loved the years at the camp and to this day
dream several times a week that I'm still living there.

My husband traveled for a living, so my daughter and I were
left alone most of the time. The only people we knew in the area
were Sonny and Bunny Stein, and we relied heavily on their hospitable nature if we needed anything. Slowly we began to venture
out to meet some of our Love neighbors, all of whom were quite
elderly at the time. I soon realized that the culture of these hearty
Scottish-Irish descendants was vanishing and needed to be preserved. My goal upon moving to Love was to know the names of
all the people living in the cabins that dotted the back roads. Little did I realize how entwined our lives would become over the
next thirty years and how much the mountain people would come
to mean to me.

Some of the first people I became friends with were Boyd and
Gladys Coffey and Boyd's brother Samuel, who lived with them.
Although twenty-five years separated us in age, Gladys Coffey will
always be one of the best friends I made here on the mountain.

She was the most amazing woman I've ever met, and nothing was too big for her to accomplish. From canning to remodeling, Gladys was always busy doing something. One snowy February morning, she called and asked me to meet her up at their camp on the next ridge over and, oh yes, bring a crowbar and a hammer. In less than three hours, Gladys, Bunny, and I had completely dismantled a small barn and had the lumber stacked in neat piles along the road. Gladys's Christian faith and unconditional love not only drew me to her but also nourished me through the bleak periods of my life. We had more good times than anyone deserves to have in a lifetime, and I look forward to spending eternity with her in heaven— catching up, swapping stories, and seeing all the sights.

Johnny and Nin Coffey lived up the road from the camp. I could not get enough of this older couple. At the time, they were both in their eighties, living alone and managing quite well. I'd walk up the path through the woods to see them every day and come back home filled with nuggets of wisdom they had unknowingly imparted to me. Trying to impress them with my newfound knowledge of canning expertise (straight from the *Ball Blue Book*), I made the mistake of telling Nin that canned jelly was good only for one year. The words no sooner were out of my mouth when Nin smiled and passed me a small mason jar filled with the most delicious strawberry jelly I'd ever smeared on a biscuit. She asked if it tasted okay and between bites of her hoecake I told her, yes, it was great. She handed me the lid and there printed on the top was the date: 1956. I would have been more mortified had it had been anyone but this patient, loving woman.

In the autumn of 1981, my neighbor Bunny Stein and I began tossing around the idea of starting a rural newspaper that could capture the stories, crafts, and culture of our mountain neighbors. The fact that neither of us had any prior experience in the newspaper business didn't daunt us one bit. We went out one day, promoting our idea, and came home with enough advertising to fund our project for one month. We decided from the beginning that we wouldn't charge anything for the paper, thus ensuring availability to the mountain people who lived on fixed incomes. By the end of Thanksgiving, we had an eight-page paper ready to take to the printer, filled with information we had gleaned from the older folks. The only thing lacking was a suitable name. We tossed around several lackluster monikers before Bunny announced, "I've got it! Backroads!" And a newspaper was born. When we brought the first edition home and saw our "bylines," it was a real head trip. But the realization that we then had to collate and fold eight thousand sheets of paper before we could deliver the first issue to the advertisers brought us down to ground level. Amid busy schedules and family obligations, we continued to crank out the newspaper for a year—interviewing people, recording the old crafts, and publishing poems and stories that had an old-time flavor.

At the end of the first year, Bunny left *Backroads,* and I was faced with the enormous decision to quit or continue on. I prayed like I had never prayed before, asking God for guidance on what He wanted me to do. I needed a cover story for my solo issue, and if one was found, I promised, with His help, to continue to publish *Backroads.* Within two days, a U.S. Forest Service employee by the name of Dave Benavitch came to my door with an envelope— material and photographs about the Civilian Conservation Corps from our area—and wanted to know if I could use it. From that moment, I never doubted that I was supposed to document the Appalachian culture as best as a rural housewife could. *Backroads* was the seed God planted in me in childhood, and it was brought to fruition by His miraculous hand at just the right time. I am convinced the Creator endows each person with a task that only they can accomplish during their time on earth. He equips us for the job even if we lack experience and confidence. As a good friend says, "The Lord doesn't always call the ordained . . . He ordains the call." The only requirement on our part is a willingness to answer that call and use our talent to honor God and bless others.

For twenty-five years, it was my privilege to talk to hundreds of mountain folk and document their lives. Everything I value the most I learned from them. The Hollywood hillbilly stereotype could not be further from the truth. Living among them, I've found the people of the Blue Ridge to be humble and giving, truthful and wise. But they are private people. Proud people. I love and defend them with everything in me. I gained an awesome respect for how they eked out a living from hardscrabble land and yet seemed to have what we all long for in this busy society. Time. Time to do a full day's work, then sit quietly on the porch at evening and listen to the whippoorwill's song. Time to visit and talk with a neighbor. Time to go to church and thank God for goodness and provision. Time to be still and listen to their own heart.

Within the pages of *Backroads*, the mountain people shared their recipes, genealogy, crafts, and lives with openness and honesty. They gave me their trust, and, in turn, I tried to be trustworthy and sensitive while writing their stories. They accepted me, an "outsider," lock, stock, and barrel and taught me well. They forgave me when I made mistakes and encouraged me when I felt defeated. Although I wrote the paper, it was never really mine. Along the way, the very people I interviewed laid claim to *Backroads,* and it became *their* paper. I was just the vessel God used to put it all together each month. It was a huge undertaking for one person, but I never tired of it. My passion for doing the job far outweighed any negatives. People asked me if I made any money publishing *Backroads*, and I told them, "No, but I've gotten rich doing it."

In the years that followed, my life took some serious twists and turns. My first marriage unraveled and came to an end. I survived a devastating house fire in which I lost everything and had to start over. But God in His infinite mercy saw fit to bring another into my life whom I could love and share my days with. One who supported not only his bride but also her mountain newspaper and the myriad things that went with it. I married my neighbor Billy Coffey in the spring of 1993, and we have had sixteen happy years together. Billy is a genuine mountain man, born in Chicken Holler and raised here in Love. His strong faith and gentle demeanor remind me daily why I fell in love with him. And, oh yes, we have built not one but *two* log cabins in our years together. The Coffey cabin is a warm and happy home, host to many friends and our five married children and six grandchildren who bring happy chaos to our lives.

The finest compliments I ever received in my quarter-century of publishing came from Doris Cash of Montebello, Virginia, and Johnny Coffey of Love. One night while roasting hot dogs over an open fire, Doris said I had given the mountain people dignity and a voice through my writing. Johnny overwhelmed me by saying, "Lynn, you write our stories exactly like they were. Why son, you're just like kinfolk."

For these reasons, I have decided to listen to my former readers and not let their stories be silenced by my retirement. It is my wish to honor the people of the Blue Ridge Mountains by compiling information from the last twenty-five years of *Backroads* and putting it in book form. I ask their forgiveness for not being able to include everyone's story in this first attempt. If it is successful, there will be others.

For all you have given, for all you have taught, I thank you. I am a blessed woman.

Backroads

1

John Massie Coffey

Love, Virginia

I f there was one resident of Love that I was closest to, it was a man by the name of Johnny Coffey. He and his wife, Nin, were my first neighbors here on the mountain and the ones I learned the most from. I have a wealth of cherished memories from this special couple, and to this day, I miss being able to run up through the woods to their home for a visit. Ninnie Virginia Coffey Coffey passed away on November 3, 1983, and Johnny lived another four years before his death on December 21, 1987. Nin was eighty-five years old at the time of her death; Johnny was a few months shy of ninety-two. These two people had the biggest impact on me with the simple way they lived and the stories they told about growing up in the mountains. It is for them that this book is written.

John Massie Coffey was born March 10, 1896, the son of Henry Thomas and Nancy Jane Campbell Coffey, whose farm was at the end of Chicken Holler. Johnny, his brother, Forest, and sister, Mary, grew up in the isolated cove, surrounded by relatives.

Chicken Holler is just across the ridge from the community of Love. If you were to follow the narrow dirt road deep into the heart of the mountain, you'd come to homesteads once owned by the Everitt, Demastus, and Coffey families. The wagon road abruptly ended at a place called Squaremouth Rocks, where Johnny's family lived. The name was derived from a small cave with a square opening that was thought to be inhabited by the early Indian tribes of the area. From Squaremouth, the only access to the nearby community of White Rock was a steep footpath that led down the mountain to the Tye River. The people of the Holler rode their horses down the path to Hercy Coffey's gristmill, where they had their corn ground into meal.

Johnny had many memories of his early years and was gracious enough to share them with those interested in knowing what life was like in the late-nineteenth and early twentieth centuries. For instance, he remembered his mother cooking in the old stone fireplace of their one-room cabin made out of round chestnut logs.

She would make the most delicious bread in her cast-iron Dutch oven. She'd work the dough into bread, and put it in the pan, and pile ashes around the bottom and on top of the lid, and let it bake until it was done. She did that with all the food we ate. Us children worked right along with our parents to put food on the table.

Our cabin had only one room with no upstairs. We had two old wooden bedsteads to sleep in, and they took up most of the room. Us smaller kids slept in what they called trundle beds, which were kept underneath the other beds during the day and then pulled out at night. Mama made homemade quilts to keep us warm. The cabin wasn't too cold in the wintertime, but it sure was hot in the summer. It had two doors but no windows at all.

When a couple got married back then, they would usually stay with either one of the parents for a while until they could save up to build their own place. Then we'd have a cabin raising. All the neighbors would turn out to help build the couple a new home. There were special men called "corner raisers" who stood on the house and saw to it the notches of the logs were made perfect so they could just roll them into place. Not everyone could do it right. Four of the best men who could do it were Gordon Everitt, Uncle Luke Demastus, Jesse Demastus, and our father, Tom Coffey. We all pitched in together and that way we got more done.

We worked hard but there was time for fun, too. When we were about seventeen years old, the game of baseball was becoming real popular. The sport came closer and closer to us until the different areas began forming their own teams and playing one another in tournaments. The

team from White Rock was already up and going when
they started looking for a place level enough to play ball
on. Our father donated a large flat piece of land near
Squaremouth Rocks as a ball field, and I guess they were
grateful because they asked Forest and me to play on
their team. We learnt the game well, and soon our team
was playing all the teams from surrounding areas. My
father played in all the practice games up at the ball field,
as we called it, and it was a great enjoyment to him.
Once, he got so wrapped up in the game that a man
came to tell him the cows were in the garden eating his
corn and my father just smiled and said, "Just play ball,
boys!"

We fellas from the White Rock team were getting better and better, until one day, we were scheduled to play
the boys from Montebello. Now Montebello had the best
team around these parts, and we were a little afraid of
them. But we went on over there and played Irish Creek
first and won 17 to 5. Later that afternoon, we played
Montebello. The captain of their team was Will Harvey,
and he told us, "You might have beat Irish Creek but you
can't do these old boys thataway." The captain of our
team was Holloway Coffey and he told us, "Just do your
best, boys."

Well, sir, we went on to beat them 3 to1 that afternoon!
It was way down in the fall of the year, and people had their
coats on, you know? When we beat them, everyone started
jumping up and down so high that their coats were flapping
up over their heads. The Montebello team swore they'd
never play us again, and do you know, they never did.

I was the pitcher in that game and Hercy Coffey was
the catcher. We made quite a pair, he and I. I had this
curve ball that no one could seem to touch. Will Harvey
asked Ashby Robertson, who was the best player on the
Montebello team, why he wasn't hitting the ball. I remember Ashby yelling back, "How can I hit it when I can't even
see it?"

Hercy and I practiced nearly every day, and we soon
got so good that a scout came from the Washington, DC,
area and tried to recruit us for the big leagues. We ended
up deciding against going, but years later, more than once
when I was out hoeing in the cornfield, I thought about
how it would have been if I had gone to play baseball in the

big leagues. So, you see, along with all the hard work, we had a lot of fun, too. But work we did.

We would cut oak and strip off the bark, and let it season and dry in order to sell it for tanbark. When it was ready, we'd put huge loads of it on a wagon and haul it down to Lyndhurst to load it on the train. We could get one cord of wood on a wagon, and it weighed about 2,300 pounds. After leaving the Holler, we hauled it with oxen up to Mountain Top Christian Church, where we'd leave it overnight. It would take us all day long just to make it that far. In the morning, we'd start out again and drive the oxen all day in order to reach Lyndhurst. Then we'd unload the bark by hand, and when we finished, we'd drive the oxen back home. It took us about two and a half days to finish the job, and then we'd divide the four dollars we got paid amongst ourselves.

Another job we had was common labor. Forest and I would get up and ride our horses over to Montebello to work ten hours digging ditches or laying rock along the road. Sometimes the temperature would be way below zero and our fingers and toes would get numb. Once we went to eat our dinner and found it was frozen solid. We did this work for a dollar and thirty-five cents a day and complained because we could only get two days of work a week. We really needed the money. Yes, son, people nowadays don't know nothing!

It was right about this time that Forest decided to marry Eva Campbell, who was born and raised in Love. Eva was sixteen years old and Forest was eighteen when they were wed in the Mountain Top Church in 1916. The old log church was located down Campbell's Mountain Road and was used until around 1921, when the congregation built a newer church at the top of the mountain where it now stands.

Forest and Eva lived with our parents in Chicken Holler about three years before buying their own place about two miles away. Earlier, our parents had built a larger cabin, which replaced the one-room log home they started out in. I followed suit and married Ninnie Virginia Coffey on July 3, 1917. Nin was a close neighbor to Eva over in Love. We lived with my parents, Forest, and Eva in the same house, and we all worked together with a minimum of fuss and helped each other along the way.

Johnny and Nin later moved into the vacant one-room log cabin of their parents and had two sons, Malcolm and Winfred, who were raised there. In the early 1930s, Johnny, who had up to that time cut timber and done common labor, began working in apples. His first job was at Homer Clark's orchard in Massie's Mill. Back then, they hauled the apples with teams of horses hooked up to large wagons. The fruit was all picked by hand and brought back to small tables set up in the field. There were no packing sheds at that time. After the apples were sorted, Johnny would load the fruit in wooden barrels, twenty-five barrels to a wagon, and drive them to Shipman, where they would be put on the Southern Railroad and shipped to their destination.

Apples weren't the only things Johnny hauled for Homer Clark. He and his crew members dug rocks out of the ground, put them on wagons, and took them to the top of a mountain where Mr. Clark was building a stone house for his family. Johnny said it took three separate teams a week to get enough rocks for the house, and they dug the basement with a horse-operated shovel. He ended up working for Clark for three years before moving on to Rose Cliff Orchard in Waynesboro. Until he saved enough money for a car, Johnny stayed at the orchard in a worker camp provided by the owner. Once he obtained a vehicle of his own, he drove back and forth from home each day. He worked at Rose Cliff until 1939, when it closed down.

By this time, Johnny had bought a 1934 half-ton Ford truck and had become an independent crew foreman for the fall apple harvest. He picked up workers and took them back home each evening. Most everyone living in the area worked for Johnny at one time or another. Tucker Snead said it best when he stated, "When Johnny started up that truck at the top of the mountain, everything from there to Sherando would climb on!"

In 1947, Johnny bought a larger truck, and in 1949, he purchased a two-ton V-8 Ford. This was the big red truck that everyone remembers best. My husband Billy said he can still remember being a child and hearing the sound of Johnny's truck coming up the Holler, wooden racks clacking back and forth, Billy's uncle Royal's three dogs chasing the truck up the road.

Early apple picking at the Wilson (Hewitt) Farm in Sherando.

Johnny kept a time log for each of the thirty to forty people who worked for him and also for the crew of ten men who helped him prune trees after the harvest was finished. He said when they got to the orchards, they would spot pick, which consisted of picking the first ripe fruit. Each worker would pick between thirty to thirty-five bushels a day. Later, when the majority of the apples ripened, each person could pick sixty bushels a day. A whole crew together might pick upward of two thousand bushels of apples a day at the various orchards. The picking season lasted from around Labor Day to the end of November and that included two pickings off each tree.

Many of the common apples at that time are now considered heirloom varieties. I had never heard names such as Red June, Parmine, Tall Sweetning, Fallow Waters, Jeanette, Limbertwig, Sheep Nose, and (Johnny's personal favorite) Black Twig. In fact, one crisp autumn day, we took Johnny on a ride to the former orchards where he worked. He asked if I'd walk into Elm Spring Orchard and ask for a man by the name of John Hannah Morris. "Tell him there's a man in the car that wants to speak to him and that he wants a Black Twig apple," instructed Johnny. I dutifully did what he asked, and when I said the man asked specifically for a Black Twig, Mr. Morris' face took on a look of recognition before asking, "Would that man in the car be Johnny Coffey?" Needless to say, a happy reunion took place in the parking lot that day.

Some of the other orchards Johnny worked at during the fifty-odd years before he retired in 1979 were: Elm Spring, White Bridge, and Willamayne in Fishersville; Seaman-Jordan in Tyro; Hayden in Crozet; Buffalo Gap in Buffalo Gap; McCue Brothers and Brooklin in Afton; Clarewin in Greenwood; Fox Hill and Hillside in Staunton; and Martin in Middlebrook.

Eventually, the Coffeys moved out of the Holler and rented the Snead place in Love. They lived in the old house until it fell into disrepair, later buying the property the home sat on plus the adjoining land. This included the acreage where the Snead School was located. A new house was built on the land, and this is where they lived for many years.

During the winter months, Johnny would go back to working in timber, cutting extract wood (still-standing dead chestnut trees) from the forests. Also, for three or four years, the state contracted the job of snow removal to Johnny. His route ran from Love to Delphine Avenue in Waynesboro, up the Howardsville Turnpike to the Blue Ridge Parkway, Reeds Gap, and back to Love. Back then, the snow was removed with a homemade wooden plow. The massive plow was about fourteen inches high with two oak boards mounted on top of one another. It was about fourteen feet in length with a wooden bar going across the middle to keep it from coming apart in heavy snows. Metal blades from a road grader were mounted on the bottom to throw snow away from the road. It was attached by thick cables to either a truck or a team of horses.

In years past, the winters in our area were much more severe, and it was nothing for snow to be on the ground from the first storm in October until spring. A three-foot snow was not an uncommon occurrence here in Love. Before the oak plow was in use, men would get together and ride their horses and mules up and down the mountain, twenty at a time, to tamp down the snow. Or they would attach a log with grabs in the ends and pull it with an animal to clear a path. So the huge wooden plow, although crude in nature, was better than anything they had had up to that point. Johnny attached the plow to the back of his 1941 ton and a half Ford truck. Later, he switched to a 1947 two-ton Ford, saying, "I've never drove anything but a Ford, son."

There were others on the mountain who helped Johnny during the winter months. Jake, Mac, and Ralph Hewitt, as well as Dewey Hite, rode with him on his route and helped load and unload the heavy plow. Ralph said he could remember, as a young boy, going with Johnny and just about freezing to death. There was never a workable heater in the truck, so an old kerosene lantern was lit and set on the floorboard. Ralph laughed at the memory of hunkering down by the lantern just to get a little warmth on his hands and coming back up with nothing but a black face from the soot. "Johnny just wasn't affected by the cold," said Ralph. "He'd just keep on going while I'd be nearly frozen through. Once, I remember seeing him under the truck putting on snow chains, and when he climbed out, he was covered up in snow. He just shook off like an old horse and asked me if I was ready to go."

Johnny and Nin standing next to their year's supply of firewood.

Johnny also did not put his trust in antifreeze, so every evening he'd drain the radiator and in the morning, refill it. This method worked as long as the truck was running. One day, after he started off the mountain, he encountered Guy Hewitt coming up the road. He pulled the truck over to the side and helped Guy hand shovel a path so he could get by. When Johnny had finished, he couldn't get the truck started again. He let it roll down the mountain, and it finally started, but he only got as far as the Mt. Torrey Furnace before it stopped. Johnny walked the two miles to his son Winfred's house where he spent the night before walking back to get the truck in the morning.

These are the memories of people who were well acquainted with the man named John Massie Coffey. I have my own memories, which I'll cherish forever. Such as when I learned how to split rounds of red oak with an eight-pound maul. I would go out early in the morning to split wood for a few hours and could hear Johnny doing the same thing up through the woods at his house. I'd chop and then he'd chop, and we would soon get a good rhythm going back and forth. By the time we'd finished, I was smiling so wide my face hurt. Then I'd walk up to his house and Nin would fix us both a cup of coffee. The way Nin drank her coffee always fascinated me, until I realized a lot of the mountain people drank it that way. She'd spoon cream and a good bit of sugar into the coffee, stir it up, and then pour the coffee from the cup into the saucer. She'd blow on it and then drink the coffee from the saucer. I never tired of watching her do it but never developed the habit myself.

One of the main things that stood out in my mind was the way Johnny called everyone "son." The first time we met him, our six-year-old daughter had on bib overalls and a Dutch boy haircut. He patted her head and called her "son." I remarked that he must have thought she was a boy. The next time it happened, I was wearing bib overalls and he called *me* son. I speculated he had vision problems. But when he called his wife son, I was stumped. Later, I came to realize he used "son" as a term of endearment for anyone he came in contact with. I now find myself using "son" for the same reason.

Johnny also was what you'd call a tomato plant aficionado, planting more than two hundred in his garden each year. He had this certain way of planting them to reap a vast crop of fruit when it came time to harvest. First, he'd dig a small hole in the soil and into that hole he'd put a shovel full of aged cow manure he'd bought from Robert Hartman, a dairy farmer who lived a few miles down the mountain. He'd then pour two small pans of water into the manure and cover it with the leftover soil. The tomatoes were then planted in the middle of these holes and 10-10-10 fertilizer was applied to the ground. He'd work in the fertilizer with a cultivating hoe worn thin from the rocky soil and then sit back and watch the 'maters grow. He was a firm believer in planting by the signs and always had a huge harvest to show for it.

John Massie Coffey in a classic pose

When Nin died in November 1983, Johnny began staying with his two sons, who lived nearby. He approached us about renting his vacant home in January 1984, and we were more than happy to oblige, since the small trailer we were occupying at the time had its drawbacks. When we said an enthusiastic "yes," Johnny asked if we'd be interested in *buying* his home. After we recovered from the mild shock of the wondrous prospect of owning the eight and a half more acres that adjoined our land, plus a very livable house, we sealed the deal and became the proud owners of our dear friend's property. It couldn't have worked out better. By selling his place to us, Johnny was relieved to know that he still had the option of "coming home" anytime he wanted. For as long as he lived, we kept his bedroom intact, and he kept his backdoor key to let himself in whenever he wanted. More than once, I'd come home from delivering the *Backroads* to find Johnny in the kitchen frying up a pan of potatoes or out in his beloved garden spot, hoeing the corn. It was an arrangement that suited everyone, and we never tired of seeing his old yellow-and-white Ford truck pull into the driveway.

When the call came on December 21, 1987, saying Johnny had passed away at his son Malcolm's home, I felt like the pegs had been kicked out from under me. I had talked to him the day before, and he was fine. Malcolm said they had been getting ready to go out Christmas shopping, and he told his dad to sit down for a minute until he cleaned up the kitchen. When he had finished, he came into the living room where Johnny was sitting and realized his dad had quietly slipped away. I remember thinking, he died just the way he lived; gently, and without a lot of fuss.

Perhaps it was because I was so young when my own grandparents died, and I never had the privilege of having a relationship with them, that I became so attached to Johnny. For whatever reason, I know when we buried him at Mountain Top Church on Christmas Eve 1987, it was the saddest day of my life. I mourned him a long time, and I still miss him after all these years. I miss his funny little laugh. The way he stood up tall and erect whenever I took his picture. And the way he patted my hand when he talked. I miss his quiet but powerful faith in God. And the way he always called me . . . "Son."

2

Butchering Hogs

Maynard Patterson and Family; Sherando, Virginia

Somewhere in the Blue Ridge Mountains, in the cold gray light before dawn, a huge scalding pan filled with fresh creek water slowly comes to a boil. With the sunrise, the age-old tradition of hog killing has begun. This ritual, which was so much a part of the early mountain culture, is now just a memory in other parts of the country. But in the smoky ridges of Virginia, the winter custom goes on. Few of the younger generation now know the art of butchering, and, indeed, there is an art to it.

In our immediate area, the Patterson family of Sherando continues the practice, making sure the butchering technique is carefully passed down to the children. Maynard said he learned the annual ritual at the knee of his own father, Charles H. Patterson. Now Dickie Patterson and his son Jamie carry on the tradition of butchering hogs, just as their forefathers did.

"Hog killin' time," as the natives call the month of December, is when a large group of neighbors gather at one another's homes for the express purpose of turning the hogs they raised into winter meat for the family. Hams, bacon, sausage, and more were made from the animals once they were killed. Butchering required many able hands to get the work done, and everyone pulled together to help one another. Families were bigger a hundred years ago, so raising six or more hogs per family was common. Pork seemed to be the number one source of meat for the mountain people, and among today's natives, that continues to be so.

For those who have never seen hog meat worked up, this chapter is not meant to offend but to show firsthand how the meat is prepared for curing, canning, or freezing. It gives a step-by-step process that will no doubt bring back memories for those who have been a part of this necessary chore. Raising hogs was a give-and-take proposition, whereby a man fed the hog for six months, and, in turn, the hog fed the man for six months.

The first thing that must be done is to kill the hog and cut its jugular vein so that the animal can bleed out. Dickie explained that to make a quick kill, you picture a cross between the hog's eyes and ears in the center of the forehead, and that's where you want to shoot. Once the hog is dead and the blood drained, it is loaded on a truck and taken to a wide wooden table with a galvanized scalding pan set up on one end. A constant fire is kept burning under the pan, and water temperature is vital to the process of scraping off the hair. If the water is too hot or too cold, it will "set" the hair into the skin, making it nearly impossible to remove. When this happens, the hair must either be shaved or singed off with fire. The optimum temperature for scraping is about 150 to 155 degrees Fahrenheit. Today, they keep track of the temperature with a thermometer, but in years past, it was a hit or miss type of thing. Most men had a knack for knowing when the water was just right, but it was a chancy operation, at best.

When the water is at the correct temperature, the carcass of the hog is lowered into the scalding pan on ropes until the hair starts to come off, usually in around five minutes time. The hog is turned over once so that both sides will scald evenly. The feet and the ears are the first things cleaned as the hog is lifted up and lain on the flat table. Then several men armed with a round metal scraping tool with a wooden handle begin stripping the hair off the body. Dickie said one of the best things to use to scrape off hog hair is an old zinc canning lid, if you can find any. The angle of the lid is perfect, but the high temperature melts and curls the edges after one or two hogs.

When the scraping is done, the hogs are then hung upside down on gambrel poles. Maynard said that years ago, they would just insert a sharp stick in the liters of the hog's back feet and hang

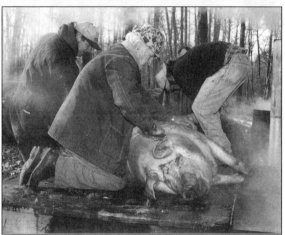

Scalding and scraping a hog

them from a tree like they do when butchering deer. Once on the poles, the hogs are washed down with hot, soapy water, getting them as clean as possible. They are rinsed several times and scraped again with the back of a knife until their bodies are pure white. Lime or ashes are sometimes added to the rinse water to help bleach the skin and aid in the removal of any remaining hair.

The head is then removed and put into a separate pan where it will be cut up and boiled down for the making of "pon-hoss," that heavenly dish that's made from meat broth, cornmeal, and the cut up organ and scrap meat from the hog.

A wheelbarrow is then pushed under the hog to catch the entrails when the animal is opened, and the heart and liver are

Hung for washing

saved for the pon-hoss or pudding meat, which is another tasty dish. The hog is then halved and taken off the pole to a clean wooden table where it is blocked out. First the lard fat is taken out. Then the fish meat (a small tenderloin attached to the backbone) is removed. The ribs are taken out next and finally the shoulders, hams, and side meat are trimmed out and put in the meat house where they will be sugar or salt cured and aged to perfection. Many people do not realize that pork chops are nothing more than the

Cutting out the rib meat

loin meat with the rib bones still attached. The remaining meat and fat are put into large tubs and ground up for sausage.

The Pattersons are set up at home for every phase of butchering. They have water as well as space and a large building in which to keep the meat, grind the sausage, and store all the equipment needed for butchering. Maynard said that in the early days, people accomplished every step of the butchering process, including rendering the lard, in one day. But today, with so many people having to work full-time jobs, the process can occur in increments over a month or so. Maynard, himself, used to wait to render his lard until several weeks after the actual butchering took place. He used the pure white lard for cooking and making lye soap.

This one animal did more to keep the people of the Blue Ridge in work and food than any other down through the years. Or as Dickie Patterson always says, "We use everything on the hog . . . but the squeal!"

3

Rendering Lard

Bobby and Robert Henderson and Junior Rhodes; Love, Virginia

One of the by-products of butchering hogs is lard, which is used for everything from cooking, seasoning cast-iron skillets, making lye soap, and waterproofing boots for the winter. And don't forget the "cracklins," which is what is left after the fat has been boiled out. Cracklins were broken up and put into cornbread, giving it a crunchy texture and flavorful taste. Lard was an essential part of the mountain diet long before fears of high cholesterol came into the picture. In fact, I have seen many of my older neighbors here in Love pour pure grease onto their meat and potatoes, much like gravy. The difference between back then and now is that we do not work as physically hard as the older generation did. We now go to offices and sit at computers all day. Our grandfathers got up from the table and went to the fields or forest, doing backbreaking jobs from sunup until sunset.

My first introduction in lard rendering took place in the early 1980s when Katie Henderson called and asked if I'd be interested in coming down to their house to take pictures of her husband Bobby and son, Robert, who were boiling down fat in their side yard. Always on the lookout for a good story for *Backroads*, I grabbed my camera and notepad and headed down the mountain. When I arrived, another neighbor by the name of Junior Rhodes was there with the Henderson men, and the fat was already boiling away in the large black kettle. The photographs that you see in this chapter are some of my favorites, and I thank

Katie for calling me that cold winter day to record this mountain tradition.

The day before, the Hendersons took the two hogs they had raised to the Farm Bureau to be killed and quartered. They used to slaughter at home, but in the last few years, they have let the Farm Bureau take over that part of the job. They then brought the meat home where it was cured, canned, or frozen. Much of it was made into fresh sausage, and the hams and side meat were cured before being wrapped in burlap sacks and hung in the barn to age. Bobby said it takes six weeks to fully cure the side meat and around six months for the hams. He learned the art of curing meat from his father and passed it on to his son, who will keep the tradition alive for yet another generation.

The first step in rendering lard is to trim the fat off the animal after it has been slaughtered. The fat is then cut into manageable chunks and put into a large container, such as a galvanized washtub. A large iron kettle is wiped out and set up off the ground so a small fire can be built under it. When it begins to heat up, "leaf" fat is added. This type of fat melts right away so that there is grease in the bottom of the kettle when the chunk-size fat is added. The chunks are stirred, and more wood is added to the fire to keep a

Boiling the fat

constant heat under the kettle. The fat, much like apple butter, has to be stirred constantly with a wooden stick to keep it from burning. It is very important to keep the fire even and not to fill the kettle too full with fat, or a grease fire can occur with disastrous results. If the fire flares up and the boiling becomes too rapid, the fat can boil over, igniting the fire like gasoline. For this reason, the lard-making process is always done outdoors. If the cracklins are boiled too long, it makes the lard dark. The idea is to watch the kettle's contents until the fat pieces themselves begin to bubble, turn golden brown and make a rattling sound.

Maynard Patterson used to add some sliced potatoes, placed in a little wire basket, to the boiling fat because he had always heard that the potatoes make the finished lard nice and white. Plus, once the raw potatoes are done cooking, they make a tasty treat while one continues to stir the pot. I once asked Maynard how long his family had been killing hogs and rendering lard and he replied, "Way back before the world was young."

Three hours into the rendering process, the cracklins are ready to take off the fire. Several layers of cheesecloth are clothes pinned to the rim of the open top of a large lard tin. Bobby explained that the tin is then placed in about three inches of water while the fat is being poured into it, or else the bottom will burst. With a small pan, the liquid fat is dipped from the kettle and poured over the cheesecloth. The cloth catches any sediment or stray cracklins and strains pure liquid fat into the lard tin. The leftover cracklins are deposited in a pillowcase spread over a five-gallon bucket to drain. When the lard tin is nearly filled to the top, the cheesecloth is taken off and attached to another empty tin and the process is repeated again and again until all the liquid and cracklins are in their proper containers.

Straining fat and cracklins from the kettle

I have to admit, when Bobby asked me if I wanted to try some of the warm cracklins, I ended up "making a pig of myself" by eating too many of the habit-forming treats. They taste just like the pork rinds you buy at the store, only more flavorful. They can also be frozen and taken out when needed. Since the hide is fried along with the fat, cracklins tend to be hard once they cool, so a metal meat hammer is used to pound them down into smaller pieces to use when making cornbread. Maynard's wife Kitty said she used about a half-pint of crushed cracklins to a big pan of skillet cornbread with delicious results.

When the liquid fat sets up, the pure white lard can be used in a variety of ways. Many times, the lard is spooned into smaller containers that can be handled more easily in the kitchen. It can be refrigerated or frozen so it won't go rancid during the hot summer months. If lard is kept too long, it develops a strong flavor, which can ruin the taste of whatever it's used for. Many years ago, people took their fat to be rendered at the cannery in Stuarts Draft. The cannery would put the liquid fat into metal cans, which were then sealed up. In this way, the lard could be stored indefinitely.

After the lard was rendered, the large kettle would be wiped out and coated with fat until it was ready to be used again. The fat would keep the kettle from rusting if stored in an outside shed.

Even though in today's culture not as many people use lard, the tradition here in the Blue Ridge Mountains continues year after year. No matter what the doctors say, potatoes fried in lard or biscuits made from the pure white fat taste better than anything that's supposed to be "good" for you. And that's a fact.

Fog in the Tye River Valley

4

Digging Ginseng

Tammy Mays; Stuarts Draft, Virginia

One of the mountain pastimes that always fascinated me was the annual end-of-summer pilgrimage to dig ginseng. Much like hunting morel mushrooms, the folks who hunt ginseng are very secretive about where they go to find the plant. Although today digging ginseng is still popular as a sport, years ago it was a big part of the mountain people's lives because many could make their living at it, and others could supplement their incomes with the valuable root, buying little extras that farm work didn't provide.

Ginseng, or "zang" as the locals call it, is a native mountain plant whose highly prized root is dug, dried, and exported to Asian countries where it is used as an alleged aphrodisiac and heart stimulant. It is also in demand here in the United States as a tonic claimed to have health benefits. The roots, when fully dried, can bring hundreds of dollars a pound. This has resulted in overcollection, and the government has now regulated when ginseng can be gathered. The plant was in danger of becoming extinct before the new laws came into effect. The collecting season in Virginia runs from August 15 through December 31, giving ample time for harvesting and then replanting the red berries, which grow in the crotch of the plant.

One person who has dug ginseng her whole life is Tammy Mays. She remembered as a young girl going with her entire family to look for "zang." It was brought home to dry and then sold to the proprietor of the Cornwall General Store for two to three dollars a pound, which was good money back then. Now, because of its scarcity, it takes a lot more effort and time to find the plant, making it more valuable.

Tammy recalled going out with nothing but a sharp stick and digging it anytime she wanted to. "It was growing all over the mountainsides, and all we had to do was go up in the woods where it was dark and moist, usually on the west side of the ridge, and dig as much as you wanted. We sold most of it but kept a little back for ourselves, too. There wasn't any better medicine than ginseng root to cure a stomachache or the cramps. We'd just chew on a little piece of it and before you knew it, the pain would go away."

Tammy said they also dug may apple, goldenseal, and lady slipper roots, but they didn't bring as much money. She said they usually dug the roots starting in the fall and gathered it right up until the time the leaves fell off. "They always said if you found a root shaped exactly like a man it would bring a big price. Ginseng reminded me of a man the way it grew; straight and tall. We'd always be on the lookout for the biggest roots we could find. You could tell what size the roots were going to be by the number of prongs the plant had on it. The more prongs, the bigger the root. We were always looking for that four- or five-prong plant 'cause we knew they would bring more money. Once I brought some of the red berries home and planted them, hoping they would grow. They did come up but later died because of the sun. Ginseng has to be planted in dark, shady, moist ground."

Ron Richardson, who was a frequent contributor of articles for the *Backroads* newspaper, also was an avid "zang" hunter. He gave more detailed information about ginseng; it is a deep-rooted, long-lived, herbaceous plant that grows in the shade of tulip poplar, walnut, basswood, and other hardwoods. It is rarely found in areas rich in pine trees. The soil is too acidic for it to thrive. It is also found in the company of black cohosh, yellow lady slipper, jack in the pulpit, trillium, wild ginger, and Solomon seal. The adult plant, eight years and older, will typically be twelve to eighteen inches tall with four stems of five leaflets each. The stems and berry stalk radiate from the same point at the top of the pencil-size plant stalk.

In September, the knot of twenty or so berries turn bright red, and by October, the leaves turn into a beautiful shade of pale golden yellow. When heavy frost burns the plants down, a scar is left on the neck at the top of the root. Counting these scars gives the approximate age of the root. Ron said the oldest one he ever found was a veteran of thirty-four years and was growing out of a crack on top of a large bolder.

Ron also gave a few conservation rules. Dig only mature roots and only after the berries are red. Be careful not to dig up the little plants, which are often found underneath the larger ones. Bury the berries one or two inches deep in the general vicinity of the mother plant. Each red berry contains two or thee flat seeds that take around eighteen months to sprout. If the seeds dry out during that time, they will not make it. Some people take the berries home with the intentions of planting them in a new location. Unfortunately, many of these seeds end up drying out in a jar and thus do not survive. If you do want to save a few berries to start a new patch, bury them in damp sand in a plastic container kept in the refrigerator. Check them often enough to make sure they don't dry out until planted. A mature ginseng plant does not flower and set seed for four or five years. Add the nearly two years it takes them to germinate, and it quickly becomes apparent why the plants are in danger of overcollection.

The first year, plants that grow from these seeds look nothing like they will as adults. They are one to two inches tall with three small triangular-shaped leaves and a skinny two-inch long root. Each year, the plant and root will grow larger, if it can survive hungry mice, land clearing, urban sprawl, floods, and "zang" hunters.

The average-sized mature root will weigh about one third of an ounce; it takes at least three ounces of green roots to make one ounce of dry.

My own memories of hunting ginseng came from Tammy Mays, who took me on several outings to find the elusive plant. Tammy had a powerful "nose" for knowing where to look for "zang," and sure enough, the two times we went up in the mountains, we came home with some roots in a bag. Some years later, my good friends John and Charlotte Hodge and I went ginsenging and came home

Ginseng leaves

with a goodly stash. I remember the day Charlotte and I drove over to Klotz Brothers in Staunton to cash in our dried roots. A bunch of men standing around in bib overalls chewing tobacco watched us come in and kind of snickered as we told the proprietor we wanted to sell some "zang." But when we dumped our roots on the scale, they quit laughing. We ate at the Chinese restaurant in Waynesboro every Sunday afternoon that entire winter on our profits!

Here are some helpful things to know if you'd like to try your hand at digging ginseng. Inquire at the Virginia Department of Agriculture and Consumer Services in Richmond to see when the season in your area starts. Obtain the appropriate permits before digging the plant on National Forest and State lands. Hunting in the Shenandoah National Park or Blue Ridge Parkway property is strictly forbidden; ginseng is completely protected on these lands.

Also, it is a good idea to go with an experienced "zang" hunter for the first few times, because there are a number of similar looking plants that might confuse the first-time hunter. Tammy dug a small ginseng plant and gave it to me so that I could correctly identify it when I saw it. She also recommended that I carry a long-handled screwdriver to dig with and a pouch or backpack to carry the roots in if I should find some. The screwdriver is very helpful in loosening the soil and for prying up rocks around the long, tuberous roots.

If you are up for a challenge and want to spend a delightful day in the great outdoors, digging ginseng may be just the ticket. Get a book on native plants to help you identify the elusive perennial, pack a lunch and some water, and be on your way!

5

Mountain Recipes

The recipes below came from most of my neighbors here in the village of Love or surrounding areas. These tried-and-true dishes have been handed down through the generations. I've incorporated them into my own family recipes and hope to pass them on to my children and grandchildren.

SKILLET CORN BREAD

William Henry Coffey gave me his recipe for corn bread, which is how the majority of the mountain people like theirs made.

1 two-inch-square chunk of lard

1½ cups self-rising yellow corn meal

2 eggs

1 cup milk

Preheat oven to 400 degrees. Put a large chunk of lard in a cast-iron skillet and melt in hot oven. Pour two tablespoons of the melted lard in the corn meal, add eggs and mix. Pour mixture into the hot skillet and bake until top is browned. Serve with real cow butter, honey, or jelly.

KATIE'S TOMATO GRAVY

*As a kid, Robert Henderson talked incessantly about his
mother's tomato gravy and how good it was. I asked Katie
for her recipe, and sure enough, Robert was right.*

2 tablespoons flour

bacon drippings

evaporated milk

water

1 pint home-canned
tomatoes

Brown two tablespoons of flour in a
skillet of bacon drippings until bub-
bly. Once the flour is browned, stir in
enough milk and water to make a
thick gravy. Drain tomatoes and add
to flour mixture. Simmer until tomatoes are soft. Serve hot with any kind
of meat, spoon over fresh biscuits, or
use bread to sop it up.

OLD TIME PICKLED BEETS

*The first time I saw anyone boiling beets outside in an iron kettle,
it was my mother-in-law, Annie Coffey. Years later, she shared
her recipe for pickled beets, and they are the best I've ever tasted.*

1 bunch fresh beets

white vinegar

5 pounds sugar
(approx., adjust to
taste)

2–3 tablespoons
pickling spice
(approx., adjust to
taste)

Pull fresh beets from the garden;
wash and cut stem ends to within
half an inch from the flesh. Do *not*
cut into the flesh, or the beets will
"bleed" and become pale. Cover with
water and bring to a boil, then simmer until fork tender. Pour off hot
water and flush with cold water until
you can handle comfortably. Skin
with your hands. Slice or cube beets
and put into a large pot. Almost
cover with white vinegar (do not add
any water), and add enough sugar
and pickling spice to suit your taste.
Heat to boiling and pack in hot jars,
adding enough juice to cover within
half an inch from jar rim. There is no
need to process in a boiling water
bath; the jars will seal by themselves.

BAKED COUNTRY HAM

*Our cousin Susie Bridge sent her recipe for cooking
a country ham, which is on most tables during the holidays.*

Trim the ham and let it soak in water for twenty-four hours.
Drain off water. Preheat oven to 500 degrees. Place ham in
roaster or other pan with a tight-fitting lid. Add hot water until
ham is half covered. Put on lid and place in the oven for thirty
minutes. Turn off oven at the end of thirty minutes, and let
stand in the oven for three hours. Turn oven on for another
thirty minutes at 500 degrees. Turn oven off at the end of this
thirty-minute period and leave ham in the oven overnight. *Do
not open oven door during the entire process!* Take out of the oven
the following morning.

EVA'S HOT MILK CAKE

*Eva Coffey submitted this old time favorite to Backroads in
the early 1980s, and I've made it many a time. It's easy to make,
and you'll usually have all the ingredients on hand.*

4 eggs

2 cups sugar

2 cups flour

1 teaspoon salt

2 teaspoons bak-
ing powder

1 cup hot milk

½ stick butter,
melted

1 teaspoon vanilla
extract

1 teaspoon lemon
extract

Preheat oven to 375 degrees. Beat eggs
first and then beat the sugar into the
eggs. Sift together the dry ingredients
and add to the egg mixture. Combine
the hot milk and melted butter and
pour into batter. Add vanilla and lemon
extract. Beat together and pour into a
tube pan. Bake for twenty-five to thirty
minutes.

FRIED APPLE PIES

This recipe came from Gladys Coffey,
my neighbor and friend in Love, Virginia.

Filling

1 package dried
apples, or use your
own

⅔ cup sugar (more
if you want it
sweeter)

¼ teaspoon salt

1 teaspoon allspice

½ teaspoon cinna-
mon

½ teaspoon nutmeg

2 tablespoons butter

To make filling: cook dried apples
until soft. Drain off liquid. Add
sugar, salt, spices, and butter. If it
needs thickening, add a little flour.
Cool.

Pastry

4 cups all-purpose
flour

1 teaspoon salt

1 teaspoon baking
powder

¼ cup sugar

¾ cup shortening

¾–1 cup milk

To make pastry: sift together flour,
salt, baking powder, and sugar in
large bowl. Add shortening and cut
in with pastry blender or two knives.
Stir in milk gradually until dough
clings together. Press dough into a
ball and roll out a quarter at a time.
Cut in five-inch circles. Put about
one and a half tablespoons of apple
filling in circle. Fold dough over to
form a semicircle. Press edges
together with a fork. Turn over and
press the other side. Pie must be
tightly sealed. Pour about two inches
of oil into a skillet and fry until
brown on both sides. Drain on paper
towel and sprinkle with sugar, if
desired. Makes about sixteen pies.

SIMPLE BERRY COBBLER

*Hallie Henderson gave me this recipe when I first moved here
in 1980, and it is good with all kinds of fruits or berries.
She said the recipe had been in her family for generations.*

1 cup milk

1 cup sugar

1 cup flour

1 teaspoon baking
powder

½ stick butter

1 quart fruit or
berries, your choice

Preheat oven to 325 degrees. Mix
milk, sugar, flour, and baking powder
to make a batter. Melt butter in a
large cast-iron skillet and pour the
batter in. Add berries or fruit and
bake until browned.

NIN'S HOMEMADE HOECAKE

*Nin Coffey was my closest neighbor in Love, Virginia. She made
a type of bread, a large biscuit called hoecake, that I had never
heard of before moving to the mountains. I soon realized it was
standard fare in the Blue Ridge. I asked for her recipe, and
she said she didn't have one. "I just make it," said Nin. I watched
her repeatedly, and this is the recipe we came up with.*

3 large handfuls of
self-rising flour (Nin
used Martha White
brand)

a three-fingered
scoop of lard

buttermilk

Preheat oven to 400 degrees. Mix
the first two ingredients together
with your fingers until all the lard is
well mixed with the flour. Add
enough buttermilk to make a sticky
dough. Turn out on a floured surface
and knead about ten times. Pull off a
piece of dough and pat into a large,
flat circle of bread. Bake for about
ten minutes or until golden brown.
Break off pieces and serve with butter, jelly, or Katie's tomato gravy (see
recipe on page 34).

EFFIE'S SWEET BREAD COOKIES

This simple, old-time treat came from Effie Demastus,
who lived across the road from us in Love.

2 cups sugar

2 cups buttermilk

5 cups flour

1 cup butter

3 eggs

Preheat oven to 350 degrees. Mix ingredients together and roll out. Cut with a biscuit cutter and bake until golden brown, about eight to ten minutes.

BREAD AND BUTTER PICKLE

This recipe was given to me by Gladys Coffey,
my best friend here on the mountain, and the one
I came to for help in the kitchen and my life.

6 onions, thinly sliced

2 green peppers, chopped

1 gallon cucumbers, thinly sliced

⅓ cup salt

3 cloves garlic (optional)

1½ teaspoons turmeric

1½ teaspoons celery seed

3 cups vinegar

5 cups sugar

Add salt to onions, peppers, and cucumbers. Cover with ice and let stand three hours. Drain salt water off. Combine the other ingredients and pour over the cucumber mixture. Bring to a boil for one minute. Ladle into hot jars and put in a hot water bath for five minutes. Save any remaining juice to make slaw. Makes about six to seven pints of pickle.

"GREENS"

"Greens" can be anything: collards, kale, mustard, turnip, dry land cress, polk, and more. They are standard fare in most every house and are served with vinegar. This is the way we fix them.

Put a goodly amount of whatever greens you want in a kettle with a little water. They will cook down almost immediately. Put a piece of country ham in for flavor or add some bacon grease and a few tablespoons of butter. Add salt and pepper to taste. A diced onion ain't bad, either! Simmer until the greens absorb the flavors.

SASSAFRAS TEA

Tea made from the roots of the sassafras tree was made each year as a spring tonic thought to cleanse the blood. In recent years, however, it was discovered the roots have a chemical property that makes drinking too much of the tea unwise. The lemony-smelling leaves can also be dried and used as a thickening agent for soups and stews. The dried powder is what is known as "filet gumbo," a key ingredient in Cajun cooking.

Dig roots of several young sassafras trees (knee-high are the easiest to dig and the most tender). Wash thoroughly and cut into pieces that will fit into a stewpot. (I peel the roots with a potato peeler to make a more concentrated infusion.) Add enough water to cover roots and bring to a boil. Cover pan and let water boil for five minutes or so. Tea should be dark red and highly aromatic. Strain roots from liquid and add honey or sugar to taste.

BROWN BEANS

Brown beans and cornbread is the number one dish here in the Blue Ridge Mountains. Even people whose diet consisted mainly of these two staples while growing up say they never tire of eating them and continue to cook a big pot of beans several times a week. Locals call them cranberry or "bird egg" beans because of their red speckled appearance. Although they look similar, brown beans are different from pinto beans. For those who don't know how to prepare them, here is a simple way to fix them.

There are two ways to soak dried beans.

The quick soak method: Put beans into a large pot with twelve cups of water and two teaspoons of salt. Boil for two minutes, then let soak in the pot for one hour. Drain and rinse before using.

The overnight soak: Place beans in a bowl with eight cups of water and one teaspoon of salt, and refrigerate them overnight. Drain and rinse before using.

For Soaking

8–12 cups water

1–2 teaspoons salt

1 pound fresh cranberry beans

OR

1 pound dried cranberry beans, sorted (to remove debris, dirt, and shriveled beans) and soaked (see above)

6 cups hot water

2 tablespoons bacon grease

2 teaspoons onion powder

1 pinch garlic salt

¼ teaspoon pepper

3 cubes chicken bullion

To cook, place the fresh or soaked beans in large pot. Add the water, bacon grease, onion powder, garlic salt, pepper, and chicken bouillon. Heat to boiling and simmer thirty minutes until tender.

Fix a pan of skillet cornbread (see recipe on page 33), pour yourself a glass of cold buttermilk, and you've got a hearty meal.

SQUIRRELS AND GRAVY

This is one of the most delicious recipes for squirrel that you can eat.
It's simple; all that's needed is to provide enough squirrels
to feed as many people as you'd like.

squirrels, 1 per person

salt, to taste

flour, for thickening

After squirrels are cleaned, quarter, halve, or leave the meat on the bones whole. Put in a pot with just enough water to cover meat, sprinkle with salt, and bring to a boil. Cover and reduce heat to a simmer. Cook until the meat is fork tender or falls off the bone. Remove meat from pot and debone. Bring broth to a boil and thicken with flour until a nice consistency of gravy is obtained. Put meat back into the gravy and serve hot over fresh-baked biscuits.

DAISY CORN PUDDING

This recipe comes from across the ridge on Reeds Gap,
where Daisy Henderson Fitzgerald lived for many years. It is
another old-time favorite with the mountain people, and you
can bet at every covered dish dinner, from church functions to
family reunions, there will be corn pudding of some sort.
Daisy's recipe is the best I've ever tasted!

1 stick butter

6 eggs

1½ cups sugar

6 tablespoons cornstarch

2 cans creamed corn

2 teaspoons vanilla

1 12-ounce can evaporated milk

Preheat oven to 350 degrees. Melt butter in a one-and-a-half-quart baking dish and set aside. Beat eggs; add sugar and cornstarch, mixing well. Add the rest of the ingredients plus melted butter and mix well. Pour into the baking dish and bake for one and one-quarter to one and one-half hours, or until center is firm and a knife comes out clean.

6

Ethna Fauber Seaman

Montebello, Virginia

I remember quite well the first time Ethna Seaman and I met. I had gone with Margie Hatter to a reunion for five ladies who had attended an old one-room school called Mill Creek near Montebello, Virginia. I was there to cover the story for *Backroads* and to interview the ladies about being early pupils at Mill Creek. As we were introduced, Ethna gave me a hard stare and gruffly stated, "We don't want no big-city reporter comin' up here writin' a bunch of lies about us!" I was so taken aback that my first instinct was to tuck tail and run. But as I stood there stuttering and trying to assure her my intentions were honorable, I saw the beginnings of an impish smile stretching across her face. That was my introduction to Ethna's sly wit and winsome ways, and it is an honor to publish her life story.

I had always admired the old Fauber homestead along the Blue Ridge Parkway near Spy Run Gap, but it wasn't until I talked to Ethna that I learned that the early farm had belonged to her grandfather, David Fauber. Just down the holler from her grandfather was another home with a large garden, barn, and springhouse. This was the home of Hampton and Rosie Virginia (Roberts) Fauber, Ethna's parents. Ethna was born there in 1904.

The land where the house sat was steep and very windy, so that same year the decision was made to move down the mountain about half a mile to a flat hollow. There was a sawmill located on the property, so Hampton Fauber and his friend Sam Groah cut

Hampton and Rosie Fauber and their ten children

and sawed the lumber for the new farmhouse off the raw materials growing on the land. Ethna was just a babe in arms when the family moved into their new place.

It was at that time that Hampton decided to rebuild the old log schoolhouse at Mill Creek with a new frame one. The school sat at the mouth of the same holler where the family lived. Education was important to the Faubers, and Ethna said it was her mother's wish that all ten of her children would learn how to read and write.

Ethna's father was a farmer who made his living through honest, hard work, and the family raised everything they needed to live right there on their farm. Her mother was kept very busy cleaning and cooking for her large brood, and Ethna remembered her ringing a little brass bell to call the children in for dinner. Years later, her mother gave the bell to the Mill Creek School, and many a teacher rang it over the years to call pupils into the classroom.

Ethna said, at one time, there were about forty children enrolled at Mill Creek School, causing her to laugh when she told me gardens weren't the only thing they grew back then—they raised a big crop of children, too. As a youngster, Ethna did her share of babysitting, saying, "Although I only had one child of my own, I must have raised forty!"

The long holler where they lived was full of other families, as well. Neighbors like the Bishops, Bradleys, Taylors, Bryants, and Ramseys dotted the mountain land and were close friends with the Faubers. Ethna's lifelong friend, Burgess Ramsey Coffey, lived at the end of the holler, under the shadow of Bald Mountain.

There is an old motto, which sums up how the Fauber family lived: "A house is made of sticks and stones, but a home is made of love alone." Ethna remembered that their home was filled with love and respect for one another. "We all worked together," she said.

Ethna remembered how her father had added special touches to their home, which made life a little easier for the whole family. "He built a wooden board-

Ethna (standing) and friends on a camping trip in the mountains

walk from the backdoor out to the barn, so we wouldn't have to get our feet muddy. He also built us a three-holer privy, which had an adult seat, a medium one for the bigger kids, and a little one for the smaller children. We also made our own whitewash in a big tub. We made it out of lime and water and then painted the house, barn, and springhouse each year. We'd also paint the trunks of our fruit trees, which helped to keep the bugs off and made them look neat and pretty."

Ethna said they would add buttermilk and bluing to the white-wash mixture and add a bit of color to make what was known as "milk paint." Reading the current country magazines, they refer to milk paint quite a bit, saying it was one of the earlier ways people added color to their homes, painting their homemade furniture with it. In today's world, antiques bring a huge price if the original paint is still intact.

At one point as we talked, Ethna got up and went to retrieve an item she wanted me to see. It appeared to be a wooden cane with long strips of folded newspaper in the handle. It was called a "fly bush," and Ethna's job as a young child was to stand on a stool and wave it across the table as the adults ate their Sunday meal. Its purpose was to keep the flies from lighting on the food.

"At times, I thought they would *never* get done eating," laughed Ethna. Early fly bushes were aptly named, because they were nothing more than a green tree limb with leaves still attached.

A big part of the mountain social life revolved around church activities. In the Montebello area, there were three churches to attend: Haines Chapel, Mount Paran Baptist Church, and the Brethren Church, all located within a short distance of one another. The different congregations mixed freely and attended the functions of each church. This is where Ethna met her husband, Wilson Seaman.

Wilson's family belonged to Mount Paran, and when they would go for services Ethna said, "We'd sit together and grin at each other." If a boy was interested in a particular girl, he would often walk her home after services and be invited to stay for the noon meal.

"Wilson and I started courting sometime in the middle 1920s. He was working in Covington at the time and would come home on the train on weekends. When he would come to see me, he would wear a blue serge suit and still straw hat. Back then, when a boy wanted to impress a girl, he would wear his Sunday best. Nowadays it is different."

Ethna said that for a man, no outfit was complete without a hat. "If a man was bare headed, it was said he was thought to be a drunk and lost it." According to Ethna, Wilson's cousin gave him some sound courting etiquette concerning his hat: when you went to see a girl, you were to "go in, tip your hat, and smile broadly. Sit down, cross your legs, and then perch your hat upon your knee." This, according to his cousin, gave you a place to hang your hat during the visit.

The young man impressed Ethna. "Wilson had enough money to buy a car, and that's when I told him he'd be worth having," laughed Ethna. "He did buy a car, too. A 1925 Model T Ford, which he paid cash for." Wilson and Ethna dated for four years before they married on February 22, 1928. They were married at the Methodist parsonage in Fairfield and had her brother Donald and her sister Mary stand up for them. After the ceremony, the couple drove to her other sister's home, in Goshen, where they spent the night.

The newlyweds lived with Wilson's parents until June of that year and then moved into a little home behind Anderson's Store in Montebello. They had three rooms downstairs and two rooms on the second floor. This is where their only child, Doris, was born. They lived there eight years before going in halves with Wilson's brother Maxie to buy Wilson's parent's place. Maxie was married to Ethna's sister, Mary, and they lived on one end of the property, while Wilson and Ethna made plans to build a home on the other end. The Seamans built their home from trees on their land, and together, using crosscut saws, they cut and shaped each piece by hand. Wilson used four-by-four-inch lumber to join the house, which Ethna said was still solid. All the window casings were hand planed, and Ethna was proud that she had had a part in helping. In her words, she accomplished three basics for Wilson: "Hand me, hold it, and go get it." When they had four walls up, they moved in, adding more rooms as they went along.

Wilson, like Ethna's father, was a farmer by trade, but during the Great Depression, he worked as a road boss on construction of Route 56. "He worked from daylight until dark for a dollar a day," recalled Ethna. "Their job was to break up the large rocks with a sledgehammer into smaller pieces for the road bed."

Wilson and Ethna worked together raising cattle and sheep, selling off the spring lambs and shorn wool as profit. They kept horses for farm work as well as pleasure riding, and Ethna could work a horse as well as any man. She remembers "Dolly" as being the last horse they kept before Wilson replaced her with a tractor.

Wilson passed away in June of 1986 and although Ethna missed him greatly, she had fond memories of their close life together and remained active in her community. She was born and raised in the Montebello area and was quite content to spend the rest of her days there.

7

Signs and Superstitions, Remedies and Cures

SIGNS AND SUPERSTITIONS

Animal Weather Predictions

If crows fly unusually high, expect high wind.

If quail sun themselves in coveys, expect three days of good weather.

If deer lose their spots by mid-July, expect an early fall.

If butterflies appear late in autumn, colder weather will come soon.

Bad Luck for Travelers

Picking up a spoon found lying beside the road.

Returning to the house after starting out on a trip, unless one counts backward from ten.

Cross Marks

It is bad luck to leave a neighbor's house by a different door from the one used to enter. If this happens, the person must make a cross on the ground, spit in the middle, and then leave through the same door he came in.

When a rabbit runs across the road in front of you, it is a bad sign. Cross yourself or make an X in the road, and spit in it; then walk backward over the place where the rabbit crossed. If a rabbit crosses the road behind you, it is a good sign; you have passed trouble.

If the right shoestring becomes accidentally untied, it is a sign that a woman is talking well about you. If it's the left shoestring, a woman is talking evil. To prevent evil, make a cross mark on the ground, put your foot on the mark, and retie the shoestring.

If you meet a stranger in the road, you must turn around, make a cross mark on the ground, and slightly change direction for good luck.

Fogs in August

Old timers say that the number of fogs in August indicate the exact number of snows for the following winter. If the fog is light, you will have light snow, and so on.

Garden-Crop Superstitions

It is lucky to plant in the "dark of the moon" root crops, such as potatoes, onions, and beets.

It is lucky to plant in the "light of the moon" above-ground crops, such as beans, tomatoes, and corn.

Seeds soaked in milk overnight make for sweeter melons.

If it rains on June 20, grapes will fall from the vine.

A big crop of peaches means a poor crop of corn or wheat.

Livestock and Animal Superstitions

Eggs set on a Sunday produce more roosters.

If a bird pecks a window or hovers around an evildoer, it's a warning to the occupant or person to mend his ways.

Horses with "white eyes" or a lot of white markings on the feet and nose aren't good.

Plant Facts

Chiggers are plentiful on yellow flowers.

Herbs to hang inside the house to ward off evil spirits are dill, St. John's Wort, vervain, yarrow, nettle, and ivy.

Signs a Girl Will Be Kissed

A redbird or bluebird flies in her path.

She puts on a man's cap or hat.

Coffee grounds in the bottom of her cup form a ring.

She makes a rhyme while talking, without planning it.

She finds a spot of dirt on her face and remembers to kiss her hand.

Signs of Rain

Tree leaves turn up, showing undersides (rain soon).

Trains or bells, not ordinarily heard because of distance, are clearly heard.

If a rooster crows at night, it will rain before morning.

The "rain crow" calls loudly in the woods.

Bees cluster near their hives.

Cream in coffee collects at the top edge of the cup.

Signs You Will Have a Visitor

If your nose itches, company is on the way.

If a woman drops her dishrag, expect a dirty visitor.

If a woman drops a fork, a man is coming; a knife, a woman.

If a rocking chair "walks" across the floor when someone is rocking in it, company is due before nightfall.

If your left hand itches, expect to receive money.

If your right ear burns, someone is talking about you.

If the joint of your thumb itches, expect an unwelcome visitor.

Superstitions about Death

It is a bad omen if a critically ill person "picks at the bed covers."

It is a bad omen if a bird flies in the house and sits on a bed.

It is bad luck if a stopped clock suddenly begins to strike.

It is a sign of coming death if a picture suddenly falls off the wall.

"Blessed are the dead that the rain falls on."

REMEDIES

Acne

Wash your face with a diaper saturated with urine.

Burns

Make a calf get up and defecate. Put the feces in a flour sack, and cover the burn with it. Leave it on until the next day, and the burn will be well.

Dog Bites

The only safe remedy for a bite from a dog suspected of madness is to burn out the wound thoroughly with a red-hot iron, or with lunar caustic, for a full eight seconds. This will destroy the entire surface of the wound. Do this as soon as possible, for no time is to be lost. It is to be expected that the parts touched with the iron will turn black.

Felon

(painful inflammation of the tisssues of a finger or toe)

Take rock salt and dry in an oven. Pound it fine and mix with spirits of turpentine in equal amounts. Put into a rag and wrap around affected parts. Keep damp with turpentine, and in twenty-four hours the felon will be dead, and you'll be cured.

Hoarseness

Take four ounces of grated, fresh horseradish, saturate it in a pint of vinegar overnight, then add a half a pint of honey, and bring it to a boil. Strain and squeeze it out, retaining only the liquid. Dose, one or two teaspoons several times a day. Very good for hoarseness, loss of voice, and all other ordinary coughs.

Ingrown Toenail

Tie a lizard liver to a leather string. Tie the string around your left ankle, and the ingrown nail will disappear in nine days.

Lotion for Itch

Mix together one ounce of sulphate of potash, one-half ounce of sulphuric acid, and one pint of water. Bathe the parts affected with the disease twice a day with this lotion, first washing the parts well with soap and water. Change clothes often, and keep the parts as clean a possible. This lotion will soon cure the itch.

Nose Bleeds

In ordinary cases, cold water applied freely to the back of the neck, the face, and snuffed up the nose will check it. Press the side of the nose with a finger for one hour, and that should staunch the flow. If these measures fail, take a piece of dry salt peter, grate it into a powder, and push it up the nostril until it is filled. This cure never fails!

Stomach Complaints

A drop of oil of peppermint, a spoonful of sugar, and hot water mixed together can soothe a stomach ache.

Catnip tea has a calming effect for any type of stomach problem and will even soothe colic in babies. Take fresh leaves and add to boiling water. Steep for a few minutes in a teacup. Take out leaves, add honey, and drink.

Hiccoughs in children are immediately stopped by giving them a lump of sugar saturated with cider vinegar. The same remedy works on adults with instantaneous success.

Toad Ointment

For sprains, strains, lame back, rheumatism, and the like: take four good-sized live toads, place in boiling water, and cook until soft and mushy. Take the toads out and boil the water down to half a pint. Add one pound of fresh-churned unsalted butter and simmer together. Add two ounces of tincture of arnica and mix well. NOTE: Some persons might think this cure hard on toads, but you could not kill them quicker any other way.

A Valuable Secret

The unpleasant odor produced by perspiration is frequently the source of vexation to gentlemen and ladies. Nothing is simpler than the removal of this odor, and at much less expense and more effectually than by the application of such costly unguents and perfumes as are in use today. It is only necessary to procure some of the compound spirits of ammonia, and place about two tablespoons in a basin of water. Washing the hands, face, arms and underarms with this mixture leaves the skin as fresh and sweet as one could wish.

Weak Ankles

Hold a raw oyster in the palm of your hand, and rub ankles until the oyster is almost rubbed away. Repeat daily at bedtime, and ankles will become stronger.

CURES

Appendicitis

Tie a leather thong around your waist, and the appendicitis will enter the thong. Take the thong, and tie it around a tree; the sickness will enter the tree, and you'll be shed of it.

Arthritis

Take a dead cat into the woods to a hollow stump that has spunk in it. Twirl the cat overhead and then toss the cat to the south. Walk away north, but do not look back.

Baldness

To cure a bald pate, smear your head with fresh cow manure.

Colic

Close the windows and doors of the baby's room, and have the father keep smoking a pipe or cigar, filling the room with smoke.

Diphtheria

Have the sick person urinate on a cup of carrot greens. Hang the greens in the northwest part of the chimney for eight days.

Freckles

To get rid of freckles, get up at five-thirty in the morning on Sunday and go outside. If there is a lot of dew on the ground, wet your hands well with it, and rub it all over your face; then turn around three times, saying each time, "Dew, dew, do, do take my freckles and wear 'em on you; dew, dew, thank you." Do not wash the dew off. Do not wash your face until the next day and the freckles will be gone.

If there is no dew, wait until the following Sunday and try again.

Lockjaw

Place a wide board on the victim's head, and hit it smartly with a hammer.

Rheumatism

These are sure cures! Just place a pan of fresh chicken droppings under the bed; or wear a new penny in each shoe; or rub snake oil and skunk oil on the afflicted joints.

Seven-Year Itch

Take hog lard and apply a coating to the affected areas. Leave it on for seven days. Don't bathe and stay away from crowds.

Sore Throat

Take a black thread, tie nine knots in it, and wear it around your neck for nine days.

Stuttering

Hit the person who is stuttering in the mouth with a raw chicken gizzard.

Wart Removal

To cure warts, cut a notch on a fig tree for every wart you have. Tell no one about it, and the warts will disappear on their own.

If there is a wart on your hand, take an onion and cut it in half.

Throw away one half, but rub the other on the wart and then bury it. When the onion rots, the wart will be gone.

To cure warts, take as many grains of corn as you have warts. Stand on a bridge and throw the corn kernels over your left shoulder, and the warts will disappear.

To cure warts, go to a graveyard and holler three times like a cat.

To cure warts, steal a dirty dishrag, rub it on the wart, and then bury it on a moonlit night; tell no one.

To cure warts, count a bud on a neighbor's peach tree for each wart you have. Leave without telling the neighbor good-bye, and the warts will be gone.

If you have warts, fill your mouth with corn, dig a hole in the ground, and spit the corn kernels in and bury them.

To get rid of a wart, tie a silk thread around it, and stick a hot needle in it.

Coffey home place in Chicken Holler

8

Chair Caning

Wilson Lawhorne, Tyro, Virginia

Wilson Lawhorne was the kind of man you were not likely to forget. There was a certain kind of peace that settled over his cozy workshop as he patiently weaved chair bottoms, that made you want to sit a spell and watch him work.

I first became acquainted with Wilson at Cornerstone Baptist Church, where my husband and I were attending services. The quiet man always had a kind word for those who spoke with him, and his face seemed to radiate a constant smile. But it was his eyes that most drew me to him. They were a clear ice blue that sparkled with enthusiasm as he talked. We could hardly believe it when someone told us that Wilson was legally blind. His eyes did not have the distant stare that many times accompanies blindness. Instead, he looked directly at you in conversation, focusing on your face as he spoke.

Our preacher, Jerry Hopkins, shared that Wilson was one of the most spiritual men he'd ever met, full of compassion and humbleness of heart. He also said this remarkable man had learned the craft of chair caning through a program geared to help handicapped persons earn a living after their sight was gone. The art of chair caning is an intricate process for anyone *with* sight, much less a blind person. I asked Wilson if I could visit his workshop and interview him while he was working, and he was gracious enough to invite me.

The morning I came to his home, I quickly realized that oft times the person we think is handicapped has a better outlook on life's difficulties than people who have all their faculties. Wilson Lawhorne was such a man. Life had not always been kind to him, yet he harbored no bitterness and gave God praise for everything he was able to accomplish.

Born on Cox's Creek in Tyro, Virginia, Wilson was one of two sons and two daughters born to John Wesley and Rosabelle Lawhorne Lawhorne. Wilson remembered one house their family lived in that had five fireplaces, which were the only source of heat and were also used for cooking.

"We put our beans and potatoes in huge cast-iron pots and skillets and cooked them over the open fire. My mama made ash cakes by raking the hot coals out of the hearth and pouring a little pile of cornmeal dough in there to cook. We'd rinse the ashes off with water when they were done, and oh, they tasted good!"

Wilson Lawhorne and Flora Fitzgerald grew up together, and her brother married his sister. When Flora was thirteen years old, she went with her brother and his wife to spend the weekend at the Lawhorne home. Even though Wilson had known her all her life, he said it was that weekend when he knew he had fallen head over heels in love with her.

"I knew exactly when I fell in love with her. I don't know how it happened, but it sure did," laughed Wilson.

They waited seven more years before eloping to Rockville, Maryland, on August 29, 1940. Flora was twenty years old and Wilson was twenty-five. The young couple lived with his parents for two years, then Flora's daddy offered to fix up an old house on his property on Cox's Creek for them to live in.

They lived there six years, until the birth of their daughter Nancy in 1948. At that point, Wilson bought a piece of property from his daddy, also on Cox Creek, and had his final home built on it.

In talking about years past, Wilson said he and his brother Herman both played the banjo. His brother played the standard

Wilson and Flora, July 1995

method, while Wilson played the claw-hammer style. He smiled as he recalled his early life.

> Both of us wished we could play like the other. I could chord a little on the guitar, but mostly it was on the banjo that I used to call attention to myself. I played for dances before I became a Christian, but afterwards, I would no longer do it.
>
> I accepted the Lord in 1938 when I was twenty-three years old. I went to a little Methodist church down in Massies Mill that was holding a revival, and the preacher, a man by the name of Mr. Hoover, seemed like he was preaching directly at me, and I felt like I couldn't get away from his eyes. At the end of his message, he said, "If you don't repent and accept Christ as your Savior, you are going straight to hell." Those were his very words and I could not forget them.
>
> Although I wasn't a bad fellow to start with, my mama and daddy taught me right from wrong, and I didn't curse or smoke, drink or run around, I realized I was still lost and couldn't be saved and go to heaven just by being

"good." As I sat there in that church, the Holy Spirit began dealing with me, and when the altar call was given, I was the first one down the isle. I ain't been perfect, but I've been growing in the Lord ever since. But it hasn't been easy. I've had a pretty hard time down through my life. I've worked hard and treated people right and the Lord would be blessing me, and then it seemed like something would happen to make it all fall apart.

During the war, I was classed as 4-F, so the government sent me to Woodrow Wilson Rehab to learn the watch-making trade. I built up a good business at home and later moved to a shop on Route 151. I was starting to make a little money when I found out I was going blind.

I first noticed it while driving at night. It continued to get worse, and I went to the doctor, where he did tests, and they diagnosed me as having retinitis pigmentosis. I had to give up my watch-making business. I also drove a school bus part time and had to give that up as well.

Through a program to aid the blind, I was sent to Butner, North Carolina, where they taught me the craft of chair caning. I learned the difficult type of weaving known as seven-step hole bottom, where you weave something called binding cane. I also learned how to weave with flat reed that makes a herringbone pattern. I loved working with the seven-step caning, but it became too difficult for me because it takes a lot of figuring. I went strictly to the flat reed weave that only takes muscles and not brains.

When you have nothing but "feel," you constantly have to check your wraps for mistakes. It takes me anywhere from three to five hours to complete one chair bottom. You have to soak the reed in water to keep it moist and pliable to work with. I tack the reed on the underside of the chair to start and then weave a pattern that calls for under one/over three, and under three/over three across the rest of the chair bottom. It just takes time. I prefer to use the three-quarter reed over the half-inch because it's stronger material and lasts longer, plus it goes faster.

While Wilson worked and talked casually, I commented on his workroom, where we were sitting. He said that Flora and Nancy kept it neat as a pin for him. The room was warm and inviting, filled with antique tools hanging from pegs and a woodstove

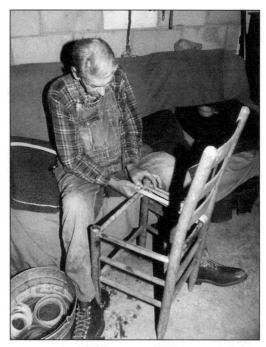

Starting to wrap the splits

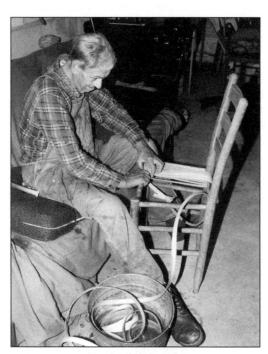

Drawing the splits tight

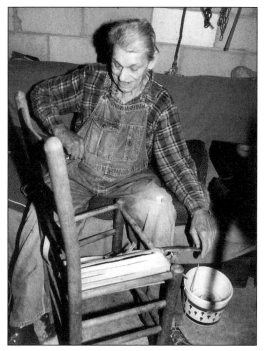

Keeping the splits moist

radiating in the corner. It was a private place where Wilson could get away and work by himself. He shared the building's history as we sat together.

In 1969, I had another outbuilding here with all my hand tools in it. In August of that year, Hurricane Camille ripped through Nelson County and swept it away. We had nothing left. The Mennonites came to help us rebuild, and they asked me how big a building I wanted. I told them I'd be satisfied with another nine-by-sixteen-foot shed, but they said they could build a twelve-by-twenty-six-foot building just as easy, and that's what they did. They installed electric lights and water and made a little wash-room for Flora. I had some yearling calves at the time, so I sold them and took the money to put in shelves, a drink box, and a snack bar. People kept coming in, and I began stocking the things they wanted. First thing you know, we had it so full you could hardly walk around it in. I went to the bank and borrowed some money for an addition.

The business grew by leaps and bounds until we had another hard lick. Flora's blood pressure started getting dangerously high, and the doctor said in order for her to live, she'd have to quit the store-keeping business. Because I had never learned Braille, I couldn't keep records, so we had to close down, and I went back to caning chairs. But I've learned not to pay too much attention to the things of this earthly life. I try to live each day like God would want me to, so that I'll be ready when Jesus comes back.

In September 1994, Wilson suffered a stroke and a heart attack, and the doctors tried to prepare him for dying. They wanted to put him on a respirator to keep him alive, and he asked the doctor, "Is that all you have left for me?" When the doctor said it was his only hope, Wilson got one of the nurses to call his preacher to come and anoint him with oil. He said, "If God heals me, fine. And if He don't, just let me die, because I am ready." The preacher came and as soon as the oil was applied, Wilson said he felt the devil trying to kill him, for his blood pressure went sky high. Jerry laid hands on him and prayed fervently. Within minutes, Wilson's blood pressure began falling until it was down to normal. "I knew God heard my prayer," said Wilson.

Wilson Lawhorne was a very special man that this world doesn't often see. He had overcome many personal hardships, yet remained hopeful and steadfast in his faith. His testimony in life makes people sit up and take notice because he lived what he preached. And for his quiet, humble testimony, I thank him.

9

Making a Kraut Mallet

Billy Coffey; Love, Virginia

One year when our garden yields were heavier than usual, we decided to make homemade sauerkraut in a crock. The only problem was that we didn't have a heavy mallet to mash the cabbage into juice. My husband Billy said he could make one for the task, and it turned out so easy, I thought it would be helpful to pass the directions on to those wishing to make one for themselves. Antique mallets can be fairly expensive to buy, so if you have access to a small hickory tree, it makes sense to simply make your own. They can be used for generations and are handy things to have around the house.

The first thing Billy had to do was to find some woods where oak and hickory trees were growing. Either one of these hardwoods make fine mallets. He cut a four-foot length of tree with no more than a four-inch diameter. (It's best to season the wood for a time, but we were in a hurry, so Billy shaped the mallet while it was still green. It did check [crack open], but that didn't hurt anything.)

Next, Billy shaved all the bark off the log with an axe. He then used a circular saw to cut manageable rounds to the depth of the handle down the log so it would be easier to trim out the handle. He cut the last round eleven inches from the bottom to form the mashing head. It's really an individual thing, and the head could be longer or shorter, depending on what you want. Since then, we've seen old mallets in antique stores that have more decorative bottoms, but ours is basic and utilitarian.

After the rounds were cut into the log, Billy took the axe and a chisel to chip off the excess wood down to the center cut, thus forming the crude handle as he worked his way down the log, being careful not to cut into the bottom end. Once this was done, he took a drawknife (a wood-working tool with a handle at each end of the blade) and worked the handle down smooth. I finished the job by sanding it with a medium-grit paper, so the up-and-down movement of

Shaving the bark off a length of hickory

mashing kraut would be easier on the hands.

Billy then took his Buck knife and carved out where the handle joined the mallet head, cutting all the little tail ends of wood out of the way. When this was finished, we had a perfectly useable

Cutting rounds to the depth of the handle

mallet with which to make our sauerkraut the next day. A homemade tool such as this will last indefinitely and can be handed down through the generations after it has served the one who made it. You don't need a lot of fancy tools or carpentry expertise to fashion one, and the price is certainly right.

In the next chapter, you will see exactly how to use the kraut mallet.

Roughing in the shape of the handle

Smoothing the handle with a drawknife

10

Homemade Sauerkraut

Billy Coffey; Love, Virginia

When I moved here thirty years ago, I began learning how to can and put up food in crocks, like the older generation had done for their whole lives. It has been a supreme joy to learn these methods of preserving food from the mountain people who willingly taught me. It is my wish to pass them down to others in the hopes that these early traditions will not perish after the elders are gone.

Johnny Coffey taught me how to make homemade sauerkraut one autumn, and although I was a little dubious of how it would turn out, I followed his directions to the letter. Two weeks later, I was rewarded with a ten-gallon crock full of crisp, tart sauerkraut that put the store-bought variety to shame. Being of German descent, good kraut was in my veins, and I canned it like my mother did, with fresh dill and caraway seed for flavor and mildness. My husband Billy and I have made kraut this way for years, and I'd like to share the simple recipe and directions in the hope that you, too, will try it for yourselves. Here it is in written and picture form to show how it's done.

The first step is to find a crock without any cracks in it. Any size will do, depending on how much kraut you want to make. We used a five-gallon crock that (after discarding the waste) made around thirteen quarts of sauerkraut. Since we didn't have a kraut mallet for pounding the cabbage, Billy made one from a length of hickory wood he cut (see previous chapter). The mallet needs to be heavy enough to mash the cabbage in the crock and make juice. You can find the old mallets in antique stores, make one yourself, borrow one, or use something equally heavy to extract the juice. Billy also made a wooden top for the crock, which needs to be weighted so that you can submerge the cabbage under its own juice. A ceramic plate will do just as well. Because of the acidic properties of the fermenting sauerkraut, do not use anything metal.

Now you are on your way to making a batch of fresh sauerkraut! Wash out the crock, and take it outside with heads of cabbage, salt, and the wooden mallet. We used eight heads of cabbage for the five-gallon crock, which didn't quite fill it up. I cut the cores out of each head and removed the outer leaves before beginning. Johnny Coffey always recommended fresh grape leaves to cover the top of the finished product, and since we live by an old hedgerow where

wild fox grapes grow, that's what we use. If you can get grape leaves, fine. If not, save some of the outer cabbage leaves and use them.

If you can borrow or buy an old-fashioned kraut cutter, that will make the job easier. If not, cut the cabbage heads crosswise, pretty thinly, as you would for slaw.

If you use a kraut cutter, place it on top of the crock so that the cabbage will fall right in. A word of warning: the blades are very sharp, so when the heads get down to fin-

Cut cabbage heads into a large crock

ger level, put another head of cabbage over the leavings and keep going.

When you get a thick layer of cut cabbage in the bottom of the crock, take the mallet and begin mashing it. Don't hit too hard, or you'll crack the crock! A steady thump-thumping will do the trick. A firm but gentle hand is the key. When the juice starts to come, add salt to taste. Personally, we don't like it really salty, so I use just enough to preserve it, but it still tastes mild. When the first layer is "slushy," put in another layer of cabbage and start mashing it into juice, adding salt to taste. Continue to cut, mash, and salt until the crock is pretty full. Make sure there is plenty of juice in it, because you'll need it later for the canning process.

When you have the crock as full as you want it, place the grape or cabbage

Begin to mash the cabbage with a kraut mallet

leaves on top of the last layer, shiny side down. Place the wooden top or plate on top of the leaves, and put a weight of some type on it. I have a washed, heavy rock that I use to submerge the kraut in its juice. Cover the crock with a dishtowel to keep the gnats and flies away, and put it in a dark, cool place for fourteen days. If you don't have a root cellar, a crawlspace or basement will do fine. Once the crock is in place, resist the urge to peek at it. It's best

*When all the cabbage is cut and mashed,
top with grape leaves*

not to bother the kraut for the full two weeks, because it disturbs the fermentation process.

At the end of fourteen days, lift the crock back outside and remove the top. Do not be grossed out by the mold and scum that has formed on the top. Simply put your hand down a few inches, lift the bad part off, and discard. I remember the first time I made kraut. Johnny was there giving me directions as we made it. Then he went home and fourteen days later called to guide me through the final process. When I lifted the lid off and saw the mold—talk about being repulsed! I told him the whole batch was ruined, but he laughed and told me to just lift off the yucky stuff, which I did. Then he told me to plunge my hand to the bottom of the crock and pull out a pinch of kraut to try. I have to admit, it looked awful and smelled pretty pungent, but I did as he asked. I'll never forget the flavor of the homemade sauerkraut. It was fabulous. A hundred percent better than anything I'd ever bought in a store.

Transfer the finished kraut from the crock into a large container, and bring it into the kitchen. You can pack it in Mason jars in two ways. For the hot-pack method: heat all the kraut at once, bringing it just to the boiling point, then pack it into hot pint or quart jars and cover with juice. You can leave it plain or add some spices. I use two heads of fresh dill and a sprinkle of caraway seeds in mine. I've heard others swear by putting a few juniper berries in it for a unique flavor. If you use the hot-pack method, the jars will seal by themselves, and there's no need to put them back into a boiling water bath.

For the cold-pack method: fill each hot jar with kraut and juice, just as in the hot-pack method. Season as you wish. Then close the jars and place them in a boiling-water bath for about fifteen minutes. They should

Put on a wooden top, and let it ferment for fourteen days

seal themselves a short time after you take them off the stove. If a jar doesn't seal, just refrigerate, and eat the kraut for supper that night.

It's true that anything homemade tastes better, but sauerkraut turns out exceptionally well. Once you try it the old-fashioned way, you'll never buy kraut from the store again. I'm sure there are more complicated methods and longer fermenting times shown in canning books, but Johnny Coffey's way has always worked for me, and it's the simplest recipe I've found.

11

Oscar Randolph Fitch

Wintergreen, Virginia

Freddie Phillips, a friend of mine from Nellysford, told me I ought to interview a black man by the name of Oscar Fitch for the *Backroads* newspaper. He said Oscar, who at that time was still working for him and other area people, would make a great article. Since Oscar didn't have a telephone, I drove over to his house one day to find out about his life and ask if he'd let me do a story on him. I found him to be a gentle and gracious man, who was more than willing to share what he knew.

The first thing that struck me about him was his appearance. Freddie had told me that Oscar was ninety-one, but I honestly could not believe that was his age. I felt sure the "elder" Fitch must be this man's father. Oscar himself assured me that he was the oldest Fitch around the Wintergreen area.

We began the interview sitting quietly on the wooden steps of the old meat house located in Oscar's backyard. He said he was born December 22, 1894, to parents Woodson and Mariah Fitch, who worked at the Phillips farm in Wintergreen. Oscar's daddy had remarried at the age of seventy-eight, and Oscar was a product of that union. So in addition to his full brothers and sisters, Oscar had four half-brothers and three half-sisters from his father's first marriage. Oscar himself worked for three generations of Phillipses: Freddie, Freddie's father, and also Freddie's grandfather. Not many men can boast of an accomplishment like that.

He was working full-time at the large Phillips farm known as

Glenthorne, when at twenty-one, he married Leona Turner of Louisa, Virginia. The couple set up housekeeping in a tiny house located on the farm and stayed there for many years before moving down the road a few miles. In 1931, the Phillips family built a home on old Route 6, and it was to there that Oscar and Leona moved and raised their family. Around the 1950s, the Fitches bought the white farmhouse for their own. The Fitches had five children, and the door was always open to any of the family that needed a place to stay. Hazel Phillips, Freddie's wife, said there was no telling how many children Oscar and his wife took in and raised. The Fitch family also survived the devastating flood that occurred in 1969 when Hurricane Camille hit the Nelson County, Virginia area. Many of their neighbors weren't as lucky.

Oscar recalled his early life in the Rockfish Valley, telling how at twenty, he became a Christian at the Elk Hill Baptist Church. "In those days, we had what was called a mourning bench, and you would kneel there until you felt changed inside," explained Oscar. "We all walked to church and I remember being baptized in the Rockfish River. The church usually did their baptizing during the first Sunday after a big revival that was held in August."

Elk Hill Baptist Church

He told of how people worked from sunup to sunset back in the old days. He also reminisced about families getting together for music and dancing when the work was done. "There was always someone who could play a banjo or a French harp, and we would make good music together."

Hunting was just as big a sport back then as it is today. The men hunted 'coons by night and squirrels by day. Oscar kept some coon dogs but did most of his hunting with Emmett Bryant, who had a lot of fine dogs.

The family raised their own hogs, and come December, they would do their own butchering. They would cure and hang the meat in the very wooden building where we sat talking. That year, Oscar said he didn't raise any hogs because "the feed got too high."

The Fitches lived off the main road, but Oscar said he enjoyed living right where he was. He had never had the urge to wander too far from where he was born and raised, saying instead that he had always been content with what he had. In talking with him, one could tell that he was happy with his life and that his roots went deep into the soil of the Rockfish Valley.

Oscar never learned how to drive a car, so he walked nearly everywhere. "I usually walk to Valleymont Market everyday, summer and winter," he said. Valleymont is the store Freddie Phillips and his family run. I asked Oscar how far away the store was from his house, and he replied, "It's two miles up and two miles back." Sitting there, talking to this elderly man, I began to see why he looked sixty-five instead of ninety-one.

As for his overall health, Oscar stated that he was very healthy. "I've never had to wear a pair of glasses in my life because I just don't need them yet. Once, when I was around seventy-one years old, I had to go to the hospital for some bladder surgery, but that didn't keep me down too long. I was back to work before you knew it. I guess it's the goodness of the Lord that's keeping me here, and I am thankful to Him for it."

Oscar tended a big garden of his own and also helped several area residents with cultivating theirs. He worked for Freddie spraying crops, working in peaches and getting in hay as needed. Longtime Wintergreen resident Bernice Spencer told me that she had delayed building a new home until Oscar could find the time to lay the foundation, knowing that if he did it, the work would be done right.

My own impression of the elder Fitch was that he was a kind-hearted, humble man, who tried to do his best in everything. But for a truer image of what kind of man Oscar really was, I asked Freddie Phillips. I think you can always tell more about a person by what their close friends say than by asking them questions about themselves. Freddie shone a beautiful ray of light on the quiet man named Oscar.

I remember when I was around ten years old. A cow had died on the farm, and the men had drug it way off down in the field so it would not be up by the house. There were large packs of wild dogs that roamed the mountains back then, feeding on the carcasses of dead animals. Our parents told us time and time again never to go near them because they were dangerous. But curiosity got the better of my brother and I one day, and we hiked down to where we knew the men had drug the cow.

Sure enough, all those dogs were there feeding on the carcass. Before we knew what really happened, the dogs saw us and headed straight for us. My brother was older and easily outdistanced me running, and as I tried to keep up with him, I slipped and fell. Before I could bat an eye, the whole pack was on top of me, biting and scratching at me.

I looked up and saw Oscar running towards me from where he was plowing, and in his hand he carried the wooden paddle that he used to clean the mud off the plow blade. He yelled at the dogs and literally beat all of them off of me and scooped me up and carried me home. My parents were so grateful that they asked Oscar to be my Godfather. That was only one incident of many in my life where Oscar deserved his title of a well-respected man.

But there are a lot of other reasons why I still continue to look up to Oscar. I can honestly say that in my sixty-five years of living, Oscar Fitch is the only man who has kept every promise he ever made to me. His word is his bond, and he is always good for it. He is the kindest, most humble Christian man I've ever met, and as far as I know, he's never said or done anything bad to anyone in his whole life. I am proud to say all these things about Oscar because I know them to all be true.

I believe Freddie's words are a perfect way to end this story about Oscar Randolph Fitch, whose family affectionately calls him by the nickname, "Joe." In a world that seems focused on glitter and wealth, Oscar knew that it's not what a man has materially that makes him successful but what he's made of on the inside that really counts. In talking with Oscar's great nephew, Bobby Fitch, he stated that his "Uncle Joe" was an exceptionally fine man who taught family members the value of living a good life. Oscar showed by his example that it is not earthly possessions that are most important to leave as a legacy but the possession of a Godly heart.

12

Churning Butter

Viola Humphreys; Blue Ridge Parkway

Although I had heard the older people talk about making butter the old-fashioned way, I had never seen or been a part of the process until Viola Humphreys asked if I'd like to watch her make it. She and her husband Lowell were the caretakers of Skylark Farm. Skylark is located at milepost 25 on the Blue Ridge Parkway, and is currently owned by Washington & Lee University in Lexington, Virginia.

The Humphreys milked their own cows, and Viola strained the raw milk for drinking purposes and churned butter out of the cream. Viola and Lowell were raised up here in the mountains, and their families had always kept cows, so both were well acquainted with the milking process. They said that the Brown Swiss, Guernsey, and Jersey cows give the milk with the most butterfat content.

The first thing Viola did after Lowell brought her the raw milk was strain it to trap debris and any stray cow hairs. She said you could use a fine metal strainer or some type of porous cloth, such as cheesecloth. The strained milk is then put into the refrigerator in covered wide-mouth gallon jars. If it's the morning milking, by evening the cream will have risen to the top of the jar. There would be approximately three to four inches of cream that Viola would skim off with a dipper and put into a separate container. I asked how to tell if you're skimming just the cream and not the milk. Viola explained that the cream is a different color, more of

Unchurned cream

pale yellow instead of pure white. She kept the cream refrigerated until she had saved at least a gallon.

When she had the required amount, she would take the container out and let it set at room temperature for a few days. The cream was then poured into some type of churn. Viola had a ceramic churn with a wooden "dasher," a long wooden handle with a flat, square bottom that is moved in an up-and-down motion to make the butter. There are also wooden butter churns, as well as smaller glass ones with an inside paddle that is hand cranked once the lid is screwed on. Electric churns are also available, but Viola said they whip the butter, making the consistency different from the hand-dashed or hand-cranked models.

The ceramic lid of the churn had a hole in the top through which the wooden dasher was inserted. Before placing the dasher in the churn, Viola would rinse its flat end in water and then the churning could begin. When asked how long it would take before the cream transformed into butter, Viola said it could vary. We

Butter gathering on the dasher

started at ten minutes after ten that morning, and I was amazed that by twenty to eleven, the butter was ready to be taken off.

I had volunteered to do the churning, and as we sat there talking congenially, Viola explained that the butter from their Brown Swiss cow is a lighter color than from some of the other breeds. She had churned butter about two to three times a week, making several pounds each time. I asked how my husband's favorite childhood treat, clabbered milk, was made. Viola said that the clotted substance came from unrefrigerated milk from which the cream had been taken and set out at room temperature until it thickened.

She told the story of her mother, Ivetta Allen Mays, making butter and wrapping it up in cheesecloth. It was then put into a gallon crock and salted before storing the container in the cold water of the springhouse. These were the days before freezers, but Viola said that butter kept this way could be preserved all winter.

As I churned, I noticed the consistency of the cream becoming much thicker. After about thirty minutes, the cream had a "slushy"

Ladling the fresh-churned butter into a dish

feel, and specks of butter began to appear on the wooden dasher handle. When Viola removed the top of the churn, the cream had suddenly become clumps of yellow butter floating in milk. Viola began to work the dasher around, calling this procedure "gathering" the butter. With a wide slotted spoon, she then lifted the butter into a clean bowl. The milk that is left is called buttermilk.

Salt was added to the clump of butter and then it was rinsed in very cold water, which brought out the rest of the milk. This was done until the water ran clear. The water was poured off, and Viola made a ball out of the butter and worked it until as much of the liquid as possible could be squeezed out. She salted to taste. If too much salt were to be added by mistake, one would only need to rinse it again and start over. I was given a teaspoon so that I could sample the finished product, and I have to say, it was delicious! Fresher and better tasting than store bought.

Viola then tore off squares of waxed paper which she laid on her kitchen counter and placed flattened balls of butter on them. The butter was wrapped and placed in the freezer. Once frozen, Viola transferred the butter from the waxed paper to Ziploc bags or

Rinsing and squeezing the butter

Butter "cakes" ready to be wrapped and frozen

Pouring off the buttermilk

Saran Wrap. When fresh butter was needed, all that had to be done was to thaw the appropriate amount.

I was really excited to be a part of Viola's butter making, but she explained with a smile that the best part was yet to come. I watched as she made several pieces of toast and then handed me one and showed me how to "sop up" the leftover butter still in the bowl. My, my, was it good. Not only did I see firsthand how easy it was to make homemade cow butter, but was rewarded with a large tub of it, along with a gallon of fresh buttermilk, to take home with me.

As I recorded the butter-making process in writing and in pho-

The finished product

tographs, Viola said it was a bittersweet day for her. Although it was my first time making butter, she explained it would be her last. They were retiring and moving to a new home, and Lowell had high cholesterol, so the family cow was to be sold. The twice-a-day milking would come to an end. How thankful I was that Viola had invited me to her house to record and preserve this old-time activity. Not many are privileged to see it in this day and age. Long live homemade cow butter!

13

Beekeeping

Howard Brydge; Reed's Gap, Virginia

oward Brydge had been a beekeeper for seventy-two years and said, "If anybody has more experience than that, I'd like to talk with him or her!"

Howard and his wife Naomi lived on one of the prettiest mountain farms in our area. The first time I rode up Reed's Gap and saw it, I thought how nice it would be to know the folks who lived there and drop by to say howdy every now and then. Little did I know that years later, I would not only be dropping by to say hello but to conduct an interview with the man who lived there.

That morning, we sat out on the porch, and Howard told me how he became a beekeeper.

I was thirteen years old when my father and I found a bee tree up on the mountain behind our house. We had a terrible time tracking the bees to their hive because we couldn't seem to find them in the air like we usually did. As it turned out, the bees were in an old hollow Chestnut tree, and they were using a small hole at the bottom as an entranceway. We couldn't see them high in the air because they were flying low to the ground in order to get into the tree.

We came back after dark one night to cut the tree and take it back to the house where we were going to set it up as a hive there. We didn't want to rob any honey from it you understand; we just wanted the whole hive. We found the tree and cut it with a crosscut saw right at ground level. When it fell, we nailed a small board on the bottom and started to cut the top off down to where the bees were located. We had to calm them down by taking an old bucket filled with smoldering rags and waving it around the tree. That's what is called "smoking" them.

Everything went along fine until my father tripped and fell off a small rock ledge on the way home, and he landed right on top of the log he was carrying. I ran home and got our neighbor, Junie Bridge, to come help my father. The next day he took him in his old road wagon to Dr. Dodge over in Stuarts Draft and found out he had some broken ribs. But even with the broken bones, we managed to get that Chestnut beehive home and set it up. And that was the beginning of my beekeeping career.

Howard told me how he went about finding a bee tree. I thought this was pretty interesting and gave me more respect for the ingenuity of the mountain people. Howard said he would go down to the creek or some other source of water and watch for some bees to appear. Bees need a constant supply of fresh water, so sooner or later, they will come to where it is. Once the bees were located, a device that would attract them was pounded into the ground. This was a small piece of wood with holes drilled into it which was nailed to the top of a broomstick, forming a T. With the broomstick in the ground, a liquid called sweet anise was poured into the holes. This was a sickly sweet substance that the bees found irresistible.

Once they found it, Howard would sit somewhere and watched them for a while. When the bees had had their fill of the anise, they would fly in a circle, higher and higher, until all at once, they would level off and fly in a straight line to their hive. That's where the old term "bee line" comes from. All that was needed was patience to see which direction they were flying. Then he'd follow them, a little at a time, taking along his anise stick and pounding it into the ground every so often so that he could keep track of their comings and goings. If he followed them long enough, they'd lead him to their bee tree, and there would be honey for the taking.

Howard said that in addition to his wild hives, he bought one from the Hamilton-Cook Hardware Store in Waynesboro and used it as a pattern for manufacturing his own hives. At one time, he had forty-nine hives on his farm property. He showed me how a hive is put together and how the bees actually make the honey. After the hive is built, the bees are ordered. They are bought by the pound, and there are fifty thousand bees to the pound, plus one queen to repopulate the hive.

A bee colony is made up of the queen, whose chief function is to lay eggs; the drones, who mate with the queen; and

A busy hive

the worker bees, who keep the hive safe and make honey. One queen is capable of laying two hundred and fifty thousand eggs per month. In a store-bought hive, she lays them in the cells of the manmade foundation, a sort of mock honeycomb that the bees enlarge and fill with honey after the eggs hatch. One queen may live up to ten years in the same hive.

The hives themselves will hold several supers (where the honey is stored) and each super is capable of holding twenty-five to thirty pounds of honey. It is possible to get sixty or more pounds of honey per hive each season, but that can vary from year to year. Honey is usually taken in the months of May or June because it's then that the bees make the most. After that time, they need it as a food supply. It takes about thirty pounds of honey for a hive to survive the winter.

Honey and comb in Mason jars

Honey color can vary according to what kind of pollen the bees are gathering. Dark honey is usually a sign that mountain wild-flowers or buckwheat was used. Lighter honey results from clover, apple, or locust blooms. Wild swarms of bees are generally more temperamental than store-bought bees, but during wet, rainy weather, all seem to be testy. Most beekeepers won't work their bees on damp days. Once the bees become accustomed to their handler, only a minimum amount of equipment is needed to work with them. Howard used a bee veil around his head and wore gloves to protect his hands. He also used a smoker, which had a calming effect on the bees.

Bees are relatively easy to maintain, but they do fall prey to the occasional bear who has a taste for honey or, worse, an illness called foul brood disease. The state sends out a man each year to check each farmer's hives; if the bees are found to have the disease, the entire colony must be destroyed lest they infect neighboring hives.

At the end of my interview, Howard recited a little poem,

which tells when to gather honey and what its net worth is after it's gathered. He said it is a good rule of thumb to follow if you are thinking about going in the bee business.

Swarm of bees in May—
Worth a load of hay.

Swarm of bees in June—
Worth a silver spoon.

Swarm of bees in July—
Isn't worth a fly.

14

Foxfire

The mountain people call it foxfire. A mysterious sight that occurs from the peaks of the Blue Ridge to the farthest shores of the ocean, causing fright in unsuspecting persons who happen across it on dark, damp nights. Perhaps you, yourself, have been out walking after dark when you came upon an eerie, glowing-green light that you couldn't identify.

Foxfire's glow is one of nature's strangest phenomena. A luminous fungus that grows on decaying wood causes its pulsing greenish glow. Thousands of phosphorescent particles in the fungus come together to make a large mass of light on whatever host it chooses. This emission of light from a living thing, such as the luminous fungus, is called bioluminescence, or "living glow," and there are many instances of it in nature.

Different kinds of mushrooms glow in the dark. Microscopic protozoa found in the oceans make water look like liquid fire when disturbed. I heard about this particular phenomenon many years ago while visiting Puerto Rico. There was a bay in the town of Ponce that was filled with phosphorescent sea life that made the water appear alive with golden luminescence. Looking at it was like watching millions of fireflies swirling in the water as the boat's wake disturbed the sea.

There are earthworms, centipedes, and snails, as well as the ever-popular fireflies, that carry their own lanterns within their bodies.

There are also certain luminous bacteria that grow on things and do not shine their light until the host dies, such as a dead fish on a beach, a cured ham that is hung in a cold, damp room, or even a human body that has been left on the battlefield.

I distinctly remember the first and only time I saw foxfire. I had just moved here and was sitting on the front porch one night during a spring rainstorm. A glowing mass in the top of an oak tree caught my eye, and I could not figure out what the eerie glow was. It was kind of spooky watching the pulsating greenish mass high in the tree. When a flashlight was aimed at the top of the branches, the light vanished. But as soon as it was switched off, the mass continued to shine. I remember that it gave me the creeps until I asked several of my neighbors what it could be. They agreed that foxfire was always seen on damp, rainy nights, so moisture obviously played a key role.

Boyd Coffey said that as a young boy, he walked down his steep lane to Frank Hatter's house to get his hair cut. It was dark when he started back home one night, and he saw a dim glow inside an old stump alongside the road. At first he thought the Arnold kids were playing a joke on him, putting a lantern inside the stump to scare him. But when he looked inside, there was nothing but a green glow. He ran all the way home, scared out of his wits. His father, Wallace, told him he had seen foxfire.

Guy Hewitt and Fred Coffey were walking home one night and spied foxfire in a large patch of skunk cabbage growing along the road just above Mr. Hatter's house. Guy said they poked at it with a stick but never could see anything, so they took off up the mountain, convinced it was a "hainted" place.

Perhaps one of these foggy, wet nights you, yourself, might be lucky enough to see . . . FOXFIRE!

Campbell home place near Spy Rock

15

The Love Post Office

Love, Virginia

In 1946, the old post office at Love, Virginia, closed its slatted window in the corner of the general store that housed it. With its demise came the end of the unique service it provided and also much of the romance surrounding the name, especially on St. Valentine's Day. That is when hundreds of people made the trip up the steep mountain to the tiny government office to have

the coveted "Love" postmark stamped on their special valentines. Or they would send the cards in separate envelopes to the Love Post Office to get them stamped and re-sent to loved ones.

First established on April 24, 1894, the post office was located in the heart of the hamlet known as Meadow Mountain. On May 15 of the same year, Hugh Coffey took the oath of office and was sworn in as the new postmaster by Wilson S. Bissell, who was the acting postmaster general at the time. Within a short time, however, the United States Postal Service was pushing for a shorter name on the postmark, since "Meadow Mountain" required too much space. Sometime that same year, Hugh's young daughter, Lovey Coffey, died of typhoid fever. So in memory of her, the village and its post office were renamed Love.

Gordon and Pearl Allen Everitt
The last postmasters at Love, Va.

Originally, the post office was incorporated into the general store Hugh Coffey operated. Although the exact date is not known, this store later burned down, and it is unknown as to whether it was rebuilt in the same location. Records show that on February 28, 1919, Gordon Everitt was appointed to the office of postmaster by Postmaster General Albert S. Burleson. The new office was then set up in Everitt's private residence and general store, the same way Hugh Coffey's was.

In the late 1920s, Gordon married Pearl Allen, a much-respected schoolteacher from that area. She not only became his wife but his assistant. In addition to their postal duties, the Everitts operated a sawmill and a gristmill. For those reasons, many times they were outside when folks came in to get their mail. They found a simple solution to the problem by hanging a police whistle on a long chain outside the store. One shrill blast on the whistle told the postmaster he had a customer waiting. Back then, people did not have house-to-house mail delivery. Instead, they were required to come to the post office.

The post office itself was a humble affair. It consisted of a corner of the store which had wooden slats built around it, with a small slot to pass the mail through. Pigeonholes made of wood housed each resident's mail, but no box numbers or names were printed on them. Gordon and Pearl knew everyone, so they had their own system of filing.

The post office served folks in surrounding areas, as well as their own community. Reed's Gap, Campbell's Mountain, and Chicken Holler residents all received their mail at the government office in Love. A simple, hand-lettered sign announced to all passing by that this, indeed, was the Love branch of the United States Postal Service.

Hand-lettered sign at the post office, 1939

In its fifty-two years of existence, there were only two postmasters who served at Love: Hugh Coffey and Gordon Everitt. There were only a handful of rural carriers serving the area for all those years. They faithfully went to and from the train station, picking up and delivering mail. The carriers, in the order in which they worked, were: Peter Coffey, F. E. Campbell, Columbus "Lum" Hatter, Andy Arnold, and Reginald Hatter. Of these men, Andy Arnold carried mail the longest. For some thirty-seven years, Andy made the long trip to the station at Lyndhurst for the incoming mail pickup. Since he lived in the Love area, he would take the outgoing mail to Lyndhurst at six o'clock in the morning and return to the Love office around noon. When the weather turned bad in the winter months, he left his Model A Ford at home and rode a horse or walked up the last steep grade to the post office. The old postman's creed, "Neither rain, nor snow, nor sleet, nor dark of night shall stay these couriers from the swift completion of their appointed rounds," was probably dedicated to the hearty souls like Andy Arnold who carried mail in the early days.

The post office at Love was classified as a fourth-class letter office, and the postmaster was paid by the number of cancellations he stamped. Around February 14, an influx of letters would arrive, many of them valentines going out to sweethearts with the special "Love" postmark, lending a romantic air to letters and cards sent out that particular day.

Inside Gordon Everitt's store. The slatted enclosure of the post office shown at right.

The village of Love is located approximately twelve miles from Lyndhurst and parallels the Blue Ridge Parkway at milepost 16. Despite the glamour and romance which its name seems to suggest, many people who have lived in this area their whole lives still do not know where Love, Virginia, is. Today, the village is sparsely populated compared to a hundred years ago. Love was once a thriving community of rugged mountain people who made their living off the rocky land. In addition to the post office, a gristmill, blacksmith shop, sawmill, two churches, and several early schools were located here. A handful of country stores where staples could be bought were in operation, since trips to the nearest town of Waynesboro were few and far between. The main road to Love was not straightened and paved until the middle to late 1940s. Up to that point, the road was nothing more than a rutted path up the mountain. I have heard many tales from the older people who remember having to walk to a neighbor's house when their old Model Ts got stuck in the mud and ask to have a mule team tow the vehicle home.

Social life in the early days consisted mostly of church services and family gatherings, where "making music" was an essential part of the visit. There were activities, too: quilting bees, apple-butter boiling, hog killing, bean and corn shelling, and house raising. When a death occurred, funerals were generally held in the home. When the service concluded, the homemade wooden coffins were hauled by horse and wagon to the church cemetery or private graveyards.

In 1939, a big change occurred with the start of construction on the Blue Ridge Parkway, and it destroyed the tranquil life of the mountain people. These people had lived their lives isolated from the onslaught of progress and the eyes of the world. Many resented the Parkway coming through private land, but knowing the inevitable, they took jobs on its construction to provide a better life for their families. With the added incomes came a restlessness of spirit to be more connected to the outside world, and the young people began leaving the mountain to seek jobs that would give them a "better" life.

When the Parkway came through the Love community, the post office had a rush of new business; it became a delivery point for the construction crews. But by the middle 1940s, the demand for rural post offices began to decline with the population. In 1946, the postmaster general came to Love one last time to collect the government stamp and postal scales that had served the village for more than fifty years. When he left, he closed the door on an era when a man could be called in from the fields by a whistle, and folks could get their letters stamped and their hearts filled . . . with LOVE.

Tyro School

16

Early Mountain Schools

Meadow, Laurel Hill, Snead, Ivy Hill, Mill Creek, Fork Mountain

An integral part of mountain life in the nineteenth and twentieth centuries was the education of its children and young people. Although the one-room schoolhouses were crude in structure, and all ages were taught different lessons within the same walls, the education remained high caliber and well equipped the pupils for everyday life.

Most of the mountain schools only went up to the seventh grade, yet many of the students opted to repeat the last grade several times to continue their learning. Looking at the content of early school exams, the children were required to learn their subjects extensively before being promoted to a higher grade.

In today's world, many complain that the classrooms are too crowded for proper learning with twenty children per class. But in the earlier centuries, sometimes there were upwards of fifty children of all ages packed inside a one-room schoolhouse. Yet the pupils seemed to get more of an education than today's kids.

Over the course of the twenty-five years that *Backroads* newspaper was published, I interviewed a wealth of people who attended these mountain schools. They were kind enough to share their experiences, along with photographs and early school documents. Each small community had its own schoolhouse, since the children who attended had to walk or ride a horse to get there. I have selected six schools close to the Love area with which to give a brief history, although there were many more in close proximity.

MEADOW SCHOOL

One of the oldest schools to serve the Love community was simply called Meadow School, probably because, at that time, the area was known as Meadow Mountain. Many of the elderly residents said this was the school their parents had attended back in the 1800s. Although I was never able to find a photograph of the school, Gordon Patterson of Sherando shared a yellowed newspaper clipping from the *Staunton Spectator*, dated 1886, in which the reporter was covering the yearly closing of this early school.

The Closing of the Meadow School
George Coffey – Editor; Sherando, Virginia
Staunton Spectator, March 1886

On the 19th instant, the patrons of Meadow School and others were called together to witness the closing scenes of their school after another prosperous session. The school was opened after singing a hymn and engaging in prayer as usual. Boys and girls were eagerly waiting a call to appear before their parents and visitors to deliver their speeches and to take part in the charades, etc., which they had prepared during the term.

The patrons and visitors were very much gratified to see the young men and ladies, and more especially the little boys and girls, stand before a large crowd and declaim with more accuracy than they anticipated that they had acquired. These exercises were continued until about 12 o'clock.

Then we assembled around the many nice things that had been prepared for dinner. Rev. J. R. Fitzgerald returned thanks for the comforts of life, which were before us. We then partook of the tempting edibles.

Then the school was called to order and addressed by different ones, among whom were Mr. Edmund Demasters, Jr., Mr. W. Tyree, who spoke on the subject, "Advice to the Young." The Rev. Fitzgerald made an able speech on "Education," showing that the subject is of deep interest to all who have a just appreciation of its merits. Final address was made by Mr. W. A. Snead, subject "The Power of an Education," showing that by gaining an education, we shall have our reward in the rich treasures of knowledge we have thus collected which shall ever be at our command, more valuable than mineral treasures.

Mr. Snead has been in charge of the school six terms in succession, and he has pleased the people better than any of his predecessors. In fact, Mr. Snead has discharged his duties so acceptably that the patrons of the school have signed a petition soliciting him to take charge of their school for the next session.

The End

LAUREL HILL SCHOOL

Laurel Hill was located about three miles down the mountain from the Love community in a field, which was part of the Ed Brydge farm, across the road from Mt. View Mennonite Church on Route 814. Built in the late 1800s, the school was thought to be a replacement for the Meadow School at the top of the mountain at Love, which had closed sometime prior.

Laurel Hill was in operation until the middle 1920s. After that, the few children remaining in the area had to walk up the mountain to the Snead School. It is unclear who actually donated the land for Laurel Hill, but it seemed to be a toss up between Ed Brydge, Jesse Bridge, and "Buzz" Henderson. Jesse Bridge was the oldest of the three who owned land there at that particular time, so it is thought that he gave the land.

To get the information about the school, I talked to Daisy Fitzgerald, her sister Marie Henderson Quick, and Marie's husband Charles Quick—three former students who attended Laurel Hill. Vera Hailey also shared a portion of her grandmother Bessie Brydge Hailey's diary, which related the early history of the school.

Regarding the structure itself, Marie said it was a one-room building with a rough weatherboard exterior. There were two windows on each side of the building and two on the back end where the teacher sat. The roof was made of chestnut shingles, and the entrance door was to the left of center as you faced the front. Looking in from the door, large blackboards lined both the back and side walls. The teacher sat at her desk at the rear, and her desk sat on an elevated platform. There was a woodstove in the middle of the room, and Charles said it was the boys' duty to make sure it was well stocked with firewood during the day. There were two wooden privies out back; one for the girls and one for the boys. The structure sat on stone pillars under each corner of the building. A split-rail fence ran past the rear of the school, which marked the boundary of the Ed Brydge farm.

Laurel Hill School and early students

The school year was only six months long back then and had classes from the first through the seventh grade. If a student wanted to go on with his education and receive a teaching certificate, he had to go to what was called a "normal," which was the equivalent of a college education, although it was only the eighth grade.

The school day started at nine o'clock in the morning and ran until three-thirty in the afternoon. The children had a half-hour lunch and two fifteen-minute recesses during the day. Classrooms contained about twenty pupils, most of whom started attending school at age six or seven.

Daisy and Marie had three other sisters who attended Laurel Hill, and out of the five, three became teachers. Bedie, the oldest, attended Bridgewater College to get her degree. Bettie went to the University of Virginia for one year. Daisy went to the eighth grade at Stuarts Draft High School for one year and boarded with the Emmett Engleman family while she studied. Marie even taught for a half session at Rankin's Creek Church, where a fifteen-pupil school was held for one year. She also filled in when needed as a substitute teacher at various schools near her home.

When the five Henderson girls attended Laurel Hill School, they walked there on a narrow mountain path that cut through the hills specifically for that purpose. They walked the path in all types of weather, and absenteeism was virtually nonexistent. The teacher was always required to be there, so most times, so were the students. If winter snows became too deep for the girls to walk in, their father, Dick Henderson, would ride ahead of them on his horse, pulling a large log behind him to clear the path.

Daisy and Marie remembered the teacher ringing a brass school bell to let the children know that classes were about to begin. When the pupils heard the bell, they lined up single file outside the door and marched into the classroom in a quiet, orderly fashion.

The day began with reading a chapter in the Bible, reciting the Lord's Prayer, and singing a song, such as a hymn or the Star Spangled Banner.

The children each had chalk and a slate on which to work their problems, and they learned to read from primers. The primers contained simple stories that became increasingly difficult as the students mastered the ones before. Daisy said they worked on one lesson each day. One she remembered went something like this:

> This is my cat.
> Her name is Sal.
> My cat is gray.
> My cat had kittens.

Each student carried his lunch to school in a one-gallon tin bucket. Everything from ham biscuits to sauerkraut and dried beans went into those lunch pails. The teacher would let the pupils warm up their meal on the woodstove. Daisy laughed at the memory of those rattling buckets sitting on top of the woodstove as they warmed.

At home, children were taught respect for their teachers, so whippings at school were rare, although standing in the corner was standard punishment for mild offenses. Charles said that they would have to stand on one foot and put their nose in the corner for ten minutes.

Recess was a time for the youngsters to go outside for a bit and run off some of their energy. Games such as "Andy over" and jump rope were common. One of the jump-rope rhymes went something like this:

> The snowflakes are silently falling, falling, falling,
> The snowflakes are silently falling, on this cold winter day.
> The little rabbits go hopping, hopping, hopping,
> The little rabbits go hopping, on this cold winter day.

I asked Charles if he played marbles at recess, and he laughed and said, "No, the boys were too busy cutting firewood for the woodstove."

Some of the early teachers at Laurel Hill School were Ina Bridge, Mae Houff, Cecil Hall, Vernie Beatty, Ruth Madison, and Susie Fitzgerald. Daisy said that Ruth Madison and Susie Fitzgerald boarded with her parents on their Reed's Gap farm.

The following excerpt, taken from Bessie Brydge Hailey's diary, gives more details of the school's history.

> There was, nearby, a one-room schoolhouse that began sometime around 1883. According to an 1884 Jed Hotchkiss map, Laurel Hill was in operation at that time. There were only six grades, with one teacher and no heating system, water cooler, or indoor rest rooms. The children or the teacher had to cut the wood and fire the woodstove, bring in a bucket of water for drinking, sweep the floors, and do all the work.
>
> Some children walked at least five miles one way to school. At recess, we played "Andy-Over" with a ball which we threw over top of the roof. We also walked on stilts and made a merry-go-round and a seesaw that we played on. Some boys cut wood during recess or skated on the ice on Back Creek, which was behind the schoolhouse.

The first teacher I remember was Miss Mae Houff. I really fell in love with her and cried when she left. Other early teachers were Miss Bessie Austin, Mrs. Inez Brydge, Olivia Raney, Miss Bedie Henderson, and Sue Fitzgerald. I finished the sixth grade at Laurel Hill in 1916. The school term was rather short, lasting between five and seven months.

Vera said her grandmother noted in her diary that she attended Sherando School in 1917, which was located five miles north of their home. In 1918, Bessie taught school, for the first time, at Laurel Hill. That year, she had approximately twenty-five students and classes went up to the seventh grade. In the fall of 1919, she went up the mountain and taught at the Snead School. Laurel Hill was still in operation in 1924, and Sue Fitzgerald was the last teacher who taught there before it closed in 1925. One of the last students to attend before it closed was Hershel Bridge, who said he started at Laurel Hill in 1920 and finished the sixth grade at Snead in 1926.

Laurel Hill stood vacant for many years, and Willie Henderson said it finally fell down from old age. He said that he remembered, as a child, going to church at Mt. View. After services were over, he would run across the road to play around the empty schoolhouse.

The days of plaited hair and slate chalkboards have drawn to a close, but the sweet memories linger on in the hearts of those who learned "Readin', Ritin', and 'Rithmetic" at Laurel Hill School.

SNEAD SCHOOL

No one knows the exact date the Snead School first existed, but the one-room log structure was deeded to the Augusta County School Board on August 19, 1896. The original deed states that the schoolhouse was already on the portion of land that was deeded from Robert A. and Nancy A. Snead in the late 1800s.

At that time, a requirement of twenty-six students per school was needed before the county would furnish a teacher. When that figure dropped below the required level, an area "volunteer" teacher, such as Marie Henderson, would have to step in. Parents

Students at the Snead School (c. 1909)

took their children's education very seriously, so they made sure that all the children were sitting in their assigned seats every day of the school year. The normal wage for teachers at that time was around twenty dollars monthly. During the 1894-95 school term, a J. S. C. Snead was on record as the teacher at Snead School.

One former student was Mrs. Gladys Snead Coffey, whose grandparents, Robert and Nancy Snead, gave the land for the school in 1896. Her parents, Lee and Florence Snead, owned the big house just up the road from the school, and they rented out rooms to the teachers who taught there. Gladys recalled:

> It was just a short walk from our house down to the school. I can still remember my first teacher, Rebecca Pannel. Other teachers I had over the years were Ruth Madison, Bessie Brydge, and Weldon Flory from Stuarts Draft. Mr. Flory was the last teacher to teach at the Snead School before it closed down. I had two sisters and a brother that attended the school, too. Although it only went up to the seventh grade, every now and then when there were a lot of older children in class; they would let us study and finish the book for eighth grade.
>
> I remember at Christmastime we would put on plays for our families, and we'd decorate a live tree with pop-

corn and paper chains to make the classroom look festive for the entertainment. At the end of the year, the teacher took us children on some type of picnic.

If we were late to class, the teacher would mark us tardy. If we got too many of these marks, we'd have to stay after school. One year, we didn't have enough children for the year, and four of us had to walk from our home at Love the three miles over to Ivy Hill School in Chicken Holler. Our teacher there was Edna Willis. She was a good teacher, but it was a long walk compared to just walking down the hill to the Snead School.

Martha Goode Coffey celebrated her ninety-first birthday in July 1983, and she was gracious enough to talk to me about her years as a student at Snead School. Martha had a lot of memories of attending there:

Back then, we used to walk the mile to school on the dirt road or on the path that ran through the woods. We started the first grade when we were seven years old and finished our schooling in the seventh grade. We only went to school five months out of the year back then.

My first teacher was Mary Snead. She was married to Zandy Snead, but then he died and left her a widow, and she taught school to earn a living for her and her little girl. I remember she boarded with the Lee Snead family during the school year.

Pupils at the old Snead School in Love, Virginia (Willie Henderson is on the left)

Our school was a one-room log cabin, and the girls sat on one side and the boys on the other. The teacher taught the little ones first, and the rest of us studied our lessons until she could get to us. We had a woodstove to keep us warm in the winter, and there was a long bench beside it so we could thaw out a bit before we started our lessons.

John Goode, Martha's father, hewed out huge oak logs and laid them across Back Creek, so the children wouldn't get their feet wet on the way to school. But Martha recalled the time she fell off the log, saying, "It was in the wintertime, and by the time I got to school, I was nearly frozen to death. I sat on that bench a long time that day!" She continued:

We used to sit two to a desk in the classroom. Usually, I sat with Callie or Elsie Snead. The boys would pull the desks back and let the girls long hair slide down between the desk and the chairs so that when they went to get up, it would jerk them back to their seats. Pure meanness!

We bought our own books and carried them home with us to study. We had a slate and chalk to do our lessons on, too. Sometimes we used pen and ink, you know. We'd dip those fine points down in the ink and write with those. If we were bad, the teacher would whip us with a switch or sit us in the corner. At times, we would have to stay after school or in at recess if we were tardy. Once I got accused of doing something I wasn't guilty of, and the teacher made me stay in at lunchtime. Oh, it upset me something terrible. I couldn't even eat my lunch!

We studied reading, writing, and arithmetic. We learned to count on a little wooden bead counter called a calculus. We had fancy Christmas programs, and on the last day of school, we always had a picnic and people came to make music for us. They would play guitars, banjos, and fiddles, and that music sounded so sweet.

I can still hear the little brass bell the teacher used to ring when school was ready to start. She would also ring it for recess and at the end of the school day, too. We went from nine o'clock in the morning until four in the afternoon. I remember I never got to finish the seventh grade because I caught the measles right at the end of the year and was too sick to finish. I always felt bad about that!

Another person who attended Snead was my neighbor Guy Hewitt. When our family bought the acre and started building a house, we couldn't figure out why we kept digging up a number of cast-iron desk parts and old glass inkwells in the foundation hole. From time to time, Guy would walk up through the woods to watch our progress. One day he said we would have to dedicate one of the corners of our new house to him alone. When we asked him why, he laughed and told us that we were digging at the site of the old Snead School, where he had spent the better part of his childhood standing in the corner.

Guy remembered starting school in September and continuing through "corn planting time," which was in May. His first-grade teacher was Becky Pannel, and he was one of the four students that Gladys mentioned who had to attend Ivy Hill when there weren't enough children for a county teacher at Snead that year.

Guy also remembered that Edna Brydge Willis was the teacher at Ivy Hill. Guy said she would ride up the mountain past his house on a big black horse named Lady and stop to pick him up on her way over to Chicken Holler. Guy was just a little fellow who was left with a permanent limp because of a bout with polio. Edna would reach down and grab his arm and swing him up behind her on the horse, and they'd ride to the Ivy School together.

Some other teachers that Guy had were Bessie Brydge, Agnes Wade, Catherine Furr, and Naomi Smoker, a Mennonite from Pennsylvania. Naomi boarded at Andy Arnold's house and walked to Snead School through the woods.

Although the first schoolhouse was constructed of logs, weatherboard was tacked on the outside sometime later, giving it a more modern look.

Guy said the first American flag he ever saw was raised at the Snead School when Miss Virginia Cox was teaching there. Florence Snead had donated the huge chestnut log that was used for the flagpole. It was cut back in the mountains and had to be hauled out with a team of mules. The large end of the pole was as big as a nail keg when it went into the ground. Guy recalled his father, Mac Hewitt, and his two brothers, Carl and Manuel, helped to set the pole, along with Hobert and Fred Coffey. When it was finally

The newer Snead School with the chestnut flagpole

lowered into the ground, it fairly towered over the schoolhouse. Every morning the flag was raised, and Miss Cox would sing the Star Spangled Banner. She would let the children take turns raising the flag, and Guy said it was always an honor to be chosen for the job.

The Snead School closed its doors around 1924, and Guy said Harry Henderson took the structure down but wasn't ever sure what he did with it. In the 1930s, the Federal Government started closing down all the one-room schoolhouses and sent buses up the mountain to pick up the children and transport them to the modern schools in town. The school at Ivy Hill was still in operation when the closedown happened.

IVY HILL SCHOOL

For many years, I listened to my neighbor, Johnny Coffey, speak about the log schoolhouse he went to as a child growing up in Chicken Holler. His father, Tom Coffey, attended the Meadow School, which had served both the Holler and the Love community. As the population grew, so did the need for two schools, and, subsequently, the Snead and Ivy Hill Schools were built. Ivy Hill served the Holler children while the Snead served Love and the surrounding areas.

I must explain the terminology of the mountain people concerning the name "Ivy." When I first moved here, it was rather confusing to me the way folks referred to the flowering shrubs rhododendron and mountain laurel, which I had identified in my Audubon wildflower book. The older people called rhododendron "laurel" and mountain laurel "ivy" or "ivory." I would try my best to correct Johnny on this misinterpretation (unsuccessfully, I might add), and finally I just gave in and called them both by their "mountain names" so people would understand what I was talking about! Where the schoolhouse was built in the holler, the hills were covered in mountain laurel, thus the name "Ivy Hill."

There were actually two Ivy Hill Schools. The first, which Johnny attended, was a one-room log structure. The second was a replacement for the original, whose logs finally rotted and fell down, and was a frame building with weatherboard siding. Both schools were built in the "flats" of the Holler, just below the present Weaver camp. They were both in the same general area but not exactly on the same spot.

I talked with Saylor and Annie Everitt Coffey, who had both attended Ivy Hill #2, and they told me about their early days there.

The school year ran from September through May. Classes started at nine o'clock in the morning and let out at three-thirty in the afternoon. Lunch was a half-hour with the standard short recesses at ten and two.

The teachers they could remember were Pettit Coffey (Saylor's older brother), Miss Pearl Allen (who became Annie's aunt when Pearl married her uncle, Gordon Everitt), and Edna Brydge (who later married Harry Willis).

The Coffey's described the school building as a frame structure with two windows on either side. The inside walls were frame with a bead-board ceiling. There were wooden desks that seated two pupils per desk. A cast-iron woodstove sat in the center of the classroom, and the stovepipe attached to it ran straight up into a brick flue to the outside. It was the parents' job to make sure there was sufficient wood cut for the long winter months.

Original Ivy Hill School in Chicken Holler (c. 1910)

There were ten to fifteen students per year, which is all that most teachers could handle. The teacher's desk sat at the front of the class on a raised platform so she could oversee everything happening in the room. A long blackboard ran along one wall.

A brass bell was rung by the teacher to signify the start of school. Bib overalls for the boys and long dresses for the girls were the standard school uniform of the day.

Punishment for laughing and out-of-turn talking was standing in the corner or being kept in at recess.

The students who attended Ivy Hill School were from the Everitt, Hewitt, Coffey, and Snead families. The Snead children began attending Ivy Hill after the Snead School closed down in 1924.

Looking back, Saylor said he walked the quarter mile to school on an old footpath that ran through the mountain up to "schoolhouse hill." The hill was so named because of the small rise of land where the school was constructed. Annie said she had farther to walk, since she lived at Love, which was about a mile away.

Just as children today, the Ivy Hill students engaged in many types of games at recess. Hide-and-seek was an all-time favorite, along with marbles, baseball, and toss the beanbag. One game, which involved the use of sticks, had the children trying to steal the other team's sticks before they were caught and thrown into "jail."

The children bought their own books to study from and, along with periodic report cards, were required to take end-of-year exams to see whether or not they could be promoted to the next grade. Ivy Hill had classes from first grade up to seventh, and many students opted to repeat the seventh for another year just to stay in school and learn more.

Ivy Hill had its share of "entertainments," which consisted of the children learning dialogs and reciting them in front of parents and friends for special occasions and at the end of the year. There was usually music at these functions, provided by local talent. Saylor recalled a Christmas entertainment that greatly amused him.

> My older brother, Pettit, came to the program dressed as Santa Claus and was trying to read his part in the play. It was getting dark so he told me to hold the lamp I was holding a little closer, so he could read better. When I put the light up to him, I accidentally caught his Santa Claus beard on fire! He ran behind the sheet we had strung across the front of the classroom and put out the fire in the beard so the little children wouldn't see. Everyone had a big laugh over it. Later in the same evening, Johnny and Forest Coffey, their sister Mary, and Dewey Fitzgerald played string music for everyone. Johnny played the fiddle, Forest and Dewey played banjos, and Mary picked the guitar. I can still remember how much we all enjoyed it.

The last teacher who taught at Ivy Hill was Thelma Jones. That was sometime in the late 1930s, after which the school closed down for good. In fact, with the closing of Ivy Hill, the whole era of one-room schools drew to a close. By the time Billy, Saylor and Annie's son, was old enough to attend school, they had to walk him the mile and a half out to the Parkway where he caught the bus bound for Stuarts Draft.

For many years after Ivy Hill closed, Houston Coffey rented the little frame building from the county and used it as a private residence. After his family moved out of the Holler, the old schoolhouse fell into disrepair and gradually went the way of so many other mountain schools . . . back to the earth.

Memories of an Ivy Hill Schoolteacher: Edna Brydge Willis

To get a different viewpoint of what school days were like at Ivy Hill, I went to the Lyndhurst home of Edna Willis, who was an early teacher there. Edna was just nineteen years of age and in her first year of teaching when the county of Nelson answered her application and assigned Edna the position at Ivy Hill.

At that time, her family lived at the base of the mountain, across the road from Mt. View Mennonite Church. Her father was Edward Brydge, and his farm is still referred to as the old Ed Brydge place, although it is no longer in the family. Edna walked the four and a half miles up the steep mountain to the school. She said there was a shortcut through the mountain back then, a narrow road. "It was right in front of the old Fred Coffey place and wound its way up to the top of the mountain and crossed the other side where Odie and Effie Demastus lived. From there it was just a short ways down the hill to the schoolhouse. Sometimes, I walked and other times, I rode my daddy's saddle horse, Lady. He had a man's Wilburn saddle, which I rode sidesaddle. In those days it wasn't considered ladylike to ride astride a horse," said Edna.

When I asked what Edna did with her horse once she got to school, she said, "On days when the weather was nice, I'd tie her to a bush and let her graze all day. If the weather was bad, I'd ride her to Forest Coffey's house and put her up in his barn for the day. Then I'd walk the rest of the way back to school."

More than a few times, Edna would pick up the little children walking to school from Love. Her favorite was little Guy Hewitt. Guy had a crippled leg and was slower walking the two and a half miles up the mountain than the other children. Edna would gently lift him up on her horse and carry him the rest of the way. Many of the other children remember her doing the same for them. Annie Coffey said many times her brother Willard was the recipient of these rides.

Recalling the school building itself, Edna said it was the second frame building she taught in. She remembered the interior pretty much the same way as Saylor and Annie Coffey did, but she also said as you walked in the door, there was a board shelf that ran from the door to the first window where a bucket of water sat with a metal dipper. The children all drank from the same dipper and used a washbasin to wash their hands before lunch. There were also nails on the back wall for the pupils to hang their coats on. Edna's mother gave her some material, and Edna made curtains for the windows.

When asked if the children ever needed discipline, Edna was quick to reply that mountain kids were the most well behaved students she ever taught.

> They thought of me as a country lady instead of a mountain lady, and for some reason, they felt that demanded more respect. But the mountain people as a whole were the most wonderful, God-fearing Christian people I've ever met, and the children were just a reflection of their parents. Whenever I made a visit to my student's homes, as a friendly call or a school-related visit, I was always ushered into the home and made to stay for a meal. In fact, once I paid a visit to the home of Winfred and Malcolm Coffey, and the weather turned bad while I was still there. Their parents, Johnny and Nin Coffey, made me spend the night with them. The parents were always most interested in their children's education and did everything they could possibly do to be helpful to the teachers who taught them.

The first year Edna taught at Ivy Hill, she had thirteen or fourteen students. The next year took her to the Pikin School near Vesuvius, where she served as teacher for one year. She remembers the school at Pikin as a two-room structure with more children. Each year, at the beginning of the new session, each pupil's weight and height was measured and logged into the school records. To weigh the children, Edna said they were marched down the road single file to the old Osceola Mill to use their scale.

In her third year of teaching, Edna was given the Ivy Hill position again. This time, she boarded with Forest and Eva Coffey, since her own family had moved to Lyndhurst. During the year Edna taught at Vesuvius, the Snead School had closed down, adding four to six more students at Ivy Hill.

Edna continued teaching for the county for just three more years before accepting a position at the Mennonite School in Stuarts Draft. There, she taught one more year, then decided to change careers and become a stenographer. She went back to school at Dunsmore Business College in Staunton to get her degree and found a job taking shorthand at the Stehli Silk Mill in Waynesboro. She worked there until she was twenty-six, then married Harry Willis. They were married fourteen months before Edna changed careers for the third time. This time to become a full-time wife and mother.

It was a long journey from studying for a teaching degree at the State Normal School for Women in Harrisonburg, which is what James Madison University was called in 1922. But Edna never forgot her experiences as a young teacher at the Ivy Hill School and the kindness of the mountain people who lived there.

MILL CREEK SCHOOL

The schoolhouse at Mill Creek lies deep in a hollow between Montebello and Dowell's Ridge and is in remarkably good condition despite its age. It now belongs to the Cash family who, in recent years, has built on an addition that comfortably holds everyone who attends the family and school reunions held there.

In writing the history of this school, I talked with Ethna and Mary Fauber Seaman of Montebello; they provided insight into what the early years at Mill Creek were like.

In 1904, Hampton Fauber, Ethna and Mary's father, decided the area needed a good school to educate their children. The county said it would provide one hundred dollars to help fund the new structure, and Mr. Fauber took it upon himself to furnish the rest of the materials and labor to build it. This was the second of two schools named Mill Creek. Like Ivy Hill, the first school was constructed of logs and served the generations of children before Ethna and Mary. The first Mill Creek was located down the hill from the present building, closer to the spring the children used for drinking water.

First-grade students started off with a primer and went on to the McGuffy readers. These early schoolbooks were of a high quality, and there was a good moral to all the stories. The adventures of Will and Nell delighted many a child learning to read.

A small brass bell was rung in the mornings to signify the beginning of class. When the pupils were settled in their seats, they said the Pledge of Allegiance, read a passage from the Bible, and recited the Lord's Prayer. Then they sang some type of hymn or a patriotic tune, such as "My Country 'Tis of Thee." Mary laughed and said that they wore this particular song very thin during the year.

The subjects of math, spelling, geography, English, and history were taught, but Ethna said they also studied physiology, which is now called anatomy. "I got my best grades in that subject," recalled Ethna.

Schoolteachers of the day were paid about forty dollars a month, and part of that paycheck went for room and board if they didn't live in the near vicinity. There were a number of different teachers over the years. Doris Fitzgerald, Della Fauber, Phineaus Abbot, "Aunt" Sally Hite, and Ethel Fauber, to name a few. The ladies remembered that Ethel Fauber always kept a switch handy for any needed discipline. But by far, a blind man by the name of Arnie Meeks was the children's favorite. Even Ethna herself taught for one term at Mill Creek. She did this after all her area neighbors signed a petition stating that they wanted her to teach their children.

Along with the studying and more serious aspects of the classroom came the funny anecdotes, which are a part of every childhood memory. Mill Creek had its share, such as the tale of two little girls who had been caught talking and sent to the corner for punishment. Each of them had to stand in the tiny corners next to the flue pipe near the woodstove. As one of them stood doing her time, she noticed some writing scratched into the wall. She inched closer to the other girl's ear and whispered, "Lookie here, the devil's been figuratin' on the wall!"

Birch twigs were cut on a regular basis and used by the children

Mill Creek School, near Montebello

as toothpicks. In one instance, Burgess Coffey was called up to the front of the class to figure a problem. While her back was turned, Ethna grabbed her birch twig and chewed it down to a stub before laying it back on her desk. When Burgess returned to her seat and saw the frayed stick, it struck her so funny that she got to laughing and couldn't quit. The teacher was young and had a good sense of humor, so infractions of this type were rarely disciplined.

Mill Creek closed in the 1940s when newer, more modern county classrooms were instituted. But the treasured memories of former students will be talked about, kept alive, and passed down to the next generation for years to come.

Reunion at Mill Creek School

In the November 1984 issue of *Backroads*, I featured a reunion of the former students of Mill Creek. Twenty years later, another reunion was held and was featured in the November 2004 edition. The men and women from the first reunion were mostly deceased, including Ethna and Mary Seaman. But students who had attended at a later date came out in abundance and provided still more remembrances. The following story has been taken from these two reunions.

Margie Coffey Hatter called me one brisk autumn morning in

October of 1984 and told me to get dressed and come over to her house in Tyro. The reason for this trip: to attend a reunion of former students of Mill Creek School.

We drove in Margie's jeep up the narrow dirt road of the North Fork toward Dowell's Ridge, where the Mill Creek schoolhouse was located. The aromas of fresh-baked biscuits, country ham, and potato salad filled the vehicle. As we bounced along the rutted road, I asked Margie questions about the early school and the people we were going to meet. I was not prepared for the nostalgic sight as we rounded the last bend, and the schoolhouse came into view.

There sat a pristine white building atop a little knoll, a plume of smoke was curling from the chimney. Walking up to the front porch, I noticed the door had a large wooden spool for a doorknob and a worn piece of wood that served as a door latch. I had to stop for a moment just to imagine all the tiny fingers that had opened that very door over the years of its existence.

As we walked inside, laughter and happy banter filled the room. People were busy laying out a huge amount of food on the long tables set up in one corner of the schoolhouse. One by one, Margie introduced me to each of the men and women who had come to that first reunion. Besides Margie's sister Lura Steele, their mother Burgess Coffey, and Burgess' sister Lena Steele, there was Hattie Grant, Wilson and Ethna Seaman, Maxie and Mary Seaman, and Inez White. Also in attendance were Rockwell Harris and Preacher Billy Morris. Together we enjoyed the covered-dish dinner and later sang hymns around the warmth of the woodstove. It was during the course of this special day that I talked to Ethna and Mary about the history of Mill Creek. The day was perfect and one I have never forgotten.

When Doris Cash (Ethna's daughter) called to say there would be a second reunion at the school, I greeted the news with great joy and much anticipation.

A lot of changes had occurred at Mill Creek since 1984. Most of the people who had come that year were gone. Ethna had left the old school to her only child, Doris, and her husband Ralph. They had added a large, two-story addition off the main room, complete with indoor plumbing. The second Mill Creek School reunion was held on August 22, 2004. Again, I talked with many of the former students, who shared their memories of the early school.

Vivian Bradley said that Lewis Bradley had cut wood for the stove to heat the new school, but she could remember that the first schoolhouse, built in the 1800s, was still standing in 1928. The first building was a small, square, wooden structure that was formerly used as a chicken coop. Vivian's grandmother and her father had attended the earlier school, along with several other family members. She was kind enough to share a list of teachers who taught at the new school from 1921 until 1940, as well as a school report from 1934–35 with twenty-one students listed.

Marie Hite Whitmore attended Mill Creek for the early grades and remembered the spring that the children drank water from. She said it was a privilege for a child to be picked to take a bucket to the spring to get drinking water for the day. "We all drank from the same dipper and nobody ever got sick," remarked Marie. She recalled the two "Johnny houses" used by the children, one for the boys, and the other for the girls. The school curriculum included reading, writing, arithmetic, history, and hygiene. In 1922, Marie went to Radford College to earn her teaching degree and later taught school in Augusta and Rockbridge Counties. She taught at Narrow Passage School from 1936 until 1939.

D. E. Hite walked to Mill Creek and remembered Anora Martin and Ethna Fauber as two of his teachers. He said there was a heating stove in the middle of the room, which kept the children warm during the cold winter months. He also said the teachers would board with Hampton and Rose Fauber, whose house was next to the school.

Lorean Falls Painter remembered that the teacher's desk stood at the front of the classroom and there were two blackboards behind her desk. On one side of the room, there were homemade wooden desks that would seat two; on the other side, newer individual desks. A large map of the world took up the back wall. When lessons were to be recited, the children had to stand in front of the class to give them.

LaRue Fauber Wilson gave me two early photos of Mill Creek students. The earliest photograph was taken around the turn of the twentieth century. LaRue's father, Hercy Fauber, and his twin sister Ethel are pictured in the back center and look to be in their late teens. Hercy has on a black bow tie and Ethel is to the right of him. LaRue still has the slate he used when he attended the first Mill Creek School. The older girl in the front row at right in the light colored dress with ruffled bottom is "Sis" Doyle, Averill Doyle's mother. The later picture was taken at the new Mill Creek School between 1937 and 1938. Lucille Allen is holding the guitar on the left, with LaRue standing next to her in the white dress. Nina Beach, the teacher that year, is standing at the top center.

Gene Bryant, seventy-two, was the youngest student who came to the reunion. He remembered that the last teacher at Mill Creek

Courtesy of LaRue Wilson

Mill Creek School students, c. 1900

was Faye Woodson and that the school closed in 1942. Gene said one time he and George Allen got into a fight, and the teacher made them apologize to each other. George did apologize but Gene wouldn't, so the teacher kept him after school that day and made him wash the blackboards and get wood in for the next day. She kept him until it started to get dark and then she walked him home.

Glenn Allen attended Mill Creek in the 1930s. He remembered that three of his teachers were Annie Harvey, Sallie Lincoln, and Nina Beach. He said Harry and Francis Phillips were two other boys who went to school there at that time.

Mill Creek students, 1937–38

These wonderful memories are all we have left of Mill Creek School's teaching days, but thanks to the Cashes, the building still stands as a gentle reminder.

FORK MOUNTAIN SCHOOL

The rich history of the Fork Mountain School in Montebello, Virginia, was gathered from old school records at the Lovingston Courthouse and from several former students. Velma Fitzgerald Ramsey and Louise Fitzgerald Seaman graciously shared their memories of what it was like being early pupils at Fork Mountain.

Located near the village of Montebello, the schoolhouse is still in remarkably good condition. Early deed records show that Lemuel Turner originally owned the property where the school was built. This was in the middle to late 1800s. Local people still refer to "Turner's Barn" on the land that now belongs to Melvin and Lois Bryant. The deed book stated that on September 1, 1890, James A. Bradley bought from the Commissioners of the Circuit Court of Nelson County a portion of land known as the Fork Mountain Tract, formerly owned by Lemuel Turner.

John J. Hill, surveyor of Nelson County, Virginia, surveyed this

Fork Mountain School (photo taken in the 1980s)

same piece of property on June 4, 1891. Bradley then sold one acre of the tract to the Massie's Mill School District #2 on which to build a school. Although there is no specific date that this sale was finalized, or the price thereof, a deed was made and entered into formal record on June 24, 1897. The acre in question was then referred to as the Fork Mountain Schoolhouse Tract. There is no date as to when the schoolhouse was built or by whom, but chances are it was in existence by the turn of the century or possibly in the late 1890s.

While browsing through different files, I came across old term reports filled out by the various teachers who taught at Fork Mountain. The earliest records were from the 1921–22 school year. The latest was from the 1944 term. In the 1921 record, a teacher by the name of Eva D. Davis was employed there. The school was in the fourth division of the Massie's Mill District. Eva taught a total of seven months and school was open for 140 days that year. The total enrollment was thirty-eight, twenty boys and eighteen girls.

By Eva's record, the school was made of pinewood. It consisted of one large open room that was in good repair. It was ventilated by the use of existing windows and a door, and was heated in the winter by a woodstove in the center of the room. There was no indoor plumbing, so an outside privy served the students and teacher alike. There were eleven oak and five pine desks and a cloth-covered blackboard measuring seven by three feet, which was in "very good condition."

The acre lot was enclosed with wire and split-rail fencing. There was no American flag on the school grounds. Grades ranged from first through the seventh. Average stay for teachers was about two years. The personal record on Eva Davis states that she was nineteen years old and taught at the Fork Mountain School for two years. She had graduated from the Macedonia School near Coffeytown, and she had a teaching certificate dated April 1917. Her salary was forty dollars a month.

Other teachers who taught at the school were Jesse J. Ponton, Marion M. Pace, Gladys M. Dameron, W. E. Cunningham, Carrie Shelton, Virginia Smith, Russell Fauber, and Susie Massie.

One of the early students at Fork Mountain was Velma Fitzgerald Ramsey. Velma related some of her experiences while attending Fork Mountain.

She started school in 1915 at the age of six. Her family lived about a mile away, and most times, she walked to and from with the other children. In the winter, she remembered that her father, Alfred Fitzgerald, would hitch his horse to a wooden sleigh and haul the children to school. On the way back, he would break a road through the snow so that the children could walk home. Velma said that even though he did this out of kindness and concern for her, she would find the biggest snowdrift and jump in it on the way home. It seems that no matter how many years go by, children are all the same!

Velma said they used chalk and slates to do their lessons, and subjects included geography, history, English, and arithmetic. She still had her old spelling book. She remembered the teacher ringing a little bell to call the pupils in for the start of class. They got a short recess during the morning hours in which to go to the bathroom or get a drink. Jim Bradley's spring provided fresh drinking water each day, and the standard bucket and common dipper were in use. They had an hour lunch break, so the children had plenty of time to eat and run off a little of their excess energy before the afternoon session began. She said they loved to play hide-and-seek and a rough-and-tumble game called "Black Horse."

Velma's favorite teacher was Jesse Ponton. She said if it hadn't been for Jesse's kindness and compassion, she doubted she would have ever gotten an education. Velma's mother died when she was just nine years old, and Velma became responsible for her youngest sister when her older sister married and moved away. The little sister was too young to attend classes so Velma decided to stay home instead of furthering her own education. Jesse made arrangements for Velma to bring the little girl to school; she could color and play while Velma did her lessons. Velma never forgot this kindness and remained close to her teacher over the years.

She laughed at the memory of Jesse, who used to wear a red flannel jumper to school and would play hide-and-seek with her students during recess. "She would hide behind a tree, and we'd all see that red jumper and catch her every time."

Term report for Fork Mountain School, 1921–22

Some of the other students who attended the Fork Mountain School were Bertha Allen, Ella Snead, Mason Bradley, Roy Snead, and Raymond Snead, who was the only boy in the sixth-grade class.

Another student who went to the school at a later date was Louise Fitzgerald Seaman. Louise started the first grade in 1942 when she was six years old. She remembered her first teacher being Hallie Cage. Louise lived about a half mile away from the school, and, like Velma, she walked to and from most days. When bad weather threatened, Louise's daddy would take the children in his big farm truck.

By the 1940s, the students had traded in their slates and chalk for paper tablets, pencils, and pens. At this time, the school still had no indoor plumbing, and the children still drank from the bucket of water with the common dipper. Louise completed all seven grades and wanted to continue her education at the nearby Fleetwood High School, but to do this, she had to board with her mother's cousin and catch the school bus that went by their home at Crabtree Falls. Louise made it through only one semester at Fleetwood before becoming so homesick that she opted to return home and repeat the seventh grade at Fork Mountain.

The last two teachers at the school were Belle Mundy and Flora Grant. With the consolidation of area schools in the 1950s, Fork Mountain closed its doors forever. The old wooden building still stands proudly along the dirt road that runs by Melvin Bryant's farm. It remains a tribute to the many children who came through its doors to learn "Readin', Ritin', and 'Rithmetic." This story is for them.

A backroad through the Blue Ridge

Nora Wilkinson

17

Diary of a Mountain Schoolteacher

The 1904 Love Story of Henry R. Mahler and Miss Nora Wilkinson

The following story was taken from the autobiography of Mr. Henry R. Mahler, who was a teacher at the Laurel Hill School during the 1904–05 school term. He met and fell in love with a young woman by the name of Nora Wilkinson, who was a teacher at the Ivy Hill School in Chicken Holler. These excerpts were provided by Mr. Mahler's son, Henry R. Mahler, Jr., who lives in Lynchburg, Virginia.

Nora Wilkinson applied for a school in Nelson County and was elected to teach in a one-room school in the Blue Ridge Mountains at Love, Virginia.

By mail, she engaged room and board at the Coffeys, who lived near the top of the mountain pass from Eastern Virginia into the Shenandoah Valley. To reach her school, she went by rail to Arrington, Virginia, where a boy in a buggy met her. It was a trip of twelve miles from the station to the Coffeys, and they did not arrive at her boarding house until late at night. She had never been in the mountains before, and the dismal night trip over rough roads made her somewhat uneasy. Her new home was a rough frame dwelling, which provided very few comforts. The house was full of children, and she had to room with the three girls of the family. Here she lived for five months, enduring the discomfort for the sake of the work she had so long dreamed of doing.

The school where she was to teach was a frame building about a mile and a half from her residence. The benches were carpenter-built, made for utility and not for comfort. Patrons of the school furnished firewood, which the older boys cut for a large stove located in the middle of the room. The older girls and the teacher swept the schoolhouse. Water was brought from a nearby spring in a bucket and placed on a shelf in the corner. There was a common dipper used by all the pupils and the teacher. There were twenty to twenty-five students. These ranged from beginners to pupils in the fifth and sixth readers. Education in this school was confined to the three R's, with spelling and some geography, history, and hygiene. Many of the children were poorly prepared and progress was slow. The attendance of some was irregular. Nora was interested in her work and for a beginner, had a successful year.

Pearl Pugh was boarding at the Snead home, a half-mile down the road from the Coffey's. She also taught at a one-room school in Augusta County, of the same general character as Nora's. Nora and Pearl soon became acquainted and being in the same kind of work, found each other congenial friends.

In those days, there was little commercial entertainment and in the mountains, none at all. The social life of the community found expression in church attendance, visiting friends and neighbors, and other such simple pastimes. In the mountain community, corn husking and apple butter boilings were popular in the early fall. When the Sneads decided to make their apple butter, young people from the whole neighborhood came to help peel apples and stir the kettle. The big kettle was made of copper and held thirty or forty gallons. It was filled three-quarters full of cider. Quartered apples gradually filled in as the cider boiled down. The apple butter was stirred with a large, narrow, hoe-shaped stirrer with a handle about ten or twelve feet long. The stirring was usually done by two people, often a young man and a young woman, one on each side of the handle. On this occasion, most of the company consisted of young boys and girls.

During the evening, while Nora and Pearl were taking their turn at the stirring, an eighteen-year-old boy appeared at the party, greeted the company, and sat down on a convenient log at some distance on the other side of the kettle from Nora and Pearl. I was that boy, Henry Richard Mahler. I was dressed in my military school khaki uniform and wore a wool hat with the brim pulled down over my eyes. The young ladies told me afterwards that they couldn't see my face too well and wondered who I was and what I looked like.

I was also a teacher at a one-room school three miles down the mountain, nearer to the Shenandoah Val-

Courtesy of Henry R. Mahler, Jr.

Henry Mahler in his Fishburne Military School uniform

ley. Some patron of my school told me there was to be an apple butter boiling at the Snead's house that night and two lady schoolteachers would be there. So I went partly for the entertainment and partly out of curiosity. It wasn't long before Mrs. Snead introduced herself and then introduced me to the girls. In a few minutes, I was helping stir apple butter, first with one girl and then the other.

We found much to talk about. Where we were from, where we had gone to school, and of course, our teaching. I found them pleasant company and probably the presence of a young man made the evening more interesting for them as well. Needless to say, I found Nora the more attractive of the two. When the apple butter was done, I escorted Nora home and then walked the three miles back to my boarding house at Mrs. Jesse Bridge's.

The three teachers became close friends. When I went to the

Sneads, Nora was usually there. When I went to the Coffeys, Pearl often went, too. Mrs. Bridge was a motherly woman and on several occasions, she invited Nora and Pearl to spend Friday or Saturday night with her so that we could all be together. Later on in the year, we put on an entertainment at Pearl's school. Pearl and I performed a dialogue. Nora and Pearl sang a duet. I sang "Old Black Joe" in costume as a solo. One of the men in the audience later said, with some justification, that I couldn't carry a tune in a bucket! Some of Pearl's pupils also had parts in the program. We had a full house and considered the evening a success, because the entertainment had given us an excuse to be together rather often for rehearsals.

As the school year advanced, I began seeing Nora more and Pearl less. Just to see her made my heart beat faster. She had a sweet disposition, was friendly, was pretty and attractive. It wasn't long before I began calling on her twice and occasionally three times a week. The walk from the Bridges to the Coffeys was six miles, but what was six miles to a young man falling in love!

Both communities must have been interested in my courtship and doubtless talked about the love affair of the two young teachers. Some young men thought they would have some fun at my expense. Twice they tried to scare me by throwing rocks from the woods as I walked home alone in the dark. On another occasion, a sheeted figure suddenly appeared before me in the road just ahead. I paid no attention to the rock throwing and walked straight up to the sheeted figure that turned out to be a young man about my own age. He was rather sheepish and admitted he was trying to scare me. From then on there were no further attempts to frighten me on my trips up and down the mountain.

Mrs. Bridge's younger daughter was attending the Stuarts Draft High School that year. At a revival in the Baptist Church, she decided to unite with that faith. Mrs. Bridge could not attend the baptismal service, so she suggested I go and take Nora with me to represent the family. I was more than willing. I secured a horse and buggy for the day. Pearl Pugh went with the daughter's sweetheart who lived near the Bridge family. There was snow on the ground and the day was cold, but we didn't mind that. We went to the morning service. From there we went to the river for the baptismal service. There were eight or ten candidates, of whom Irene Bridge was one. We took dinner with the lady with whom Irene boarded, with the minister and his wife being guests at the meal.

The length of the drive was the best feature, as far as we were concerned. We had plenty to talk about. We even discussed immersion, for Nora was a Baptist and I a Presbyterian. We were supposed to stop at Mrs. Bridge's to pick up Pearl and take her with us the rest of the way to the Sneads. We were so absorbed in each other that we forgot about Pearl and drove to the Coffeys without her. When I got back to the Bridge house, there sat Pearl waiting and wondering what had become of us. When I admitted that I had taken Nora home and had forgotten her, I had an unpleasant five minutes. Pearl was very upset and had a right to be. Young folks in love usually forget everybody except themselves, as we had done. We did get Pearl home that evening. I remember her saying she could forgive but never forget.

By this time, the reader must have reached his own conclusion about the state of my heart and mind. It was not long before I declared myself. My declaration was no masterpiece in the way of a proposal. I only said, "I love you" and "Do you love me?" Nora's answer was a rather breathless, "Yes." In my ignorance of the conventions, I concluded that we were engaged, but later I found that Nora was uncertain about the engagement part. We soon came to an understanding and began a five-year engagement period. We took Pearl into our confidence, and she seemed glad to share in our happiness. My ignorance of social conventions caused me to make another mistake. I gave Nora a ring, but it was a plain gold band, which she still wears. I did not know the distinction between an engagement ring and a wedding ring. In fact, engagement rings were not a sine qua non as they are today.

After this, most of my visits were with Nora alone in the Coffey's front room. At nine o'clock, Mr. Coffey always appeared at the door and called bedtime. That was my signal to say good night and take my departure. My frequent visits were soon to end. The school term was nearly over. We reluctantly said goodbye at the close of school at the end of February. Nora returned home, and I went to Washington and Lee for the spring term.

Thus began a long period of correspondence. We generally wrote each other two letters a week. Nora's letters were much treasured. I kept them all. We found we could express our deepest feeling in letters better than by word of mouth. So our love grew and ripened until the day of our marriage.

The next year, Nora taught at Arbor Hill in Augusta County. Since Arbor Hill was only about forty miles from Lexington, we had the opportunity of seeing each other two or three times during the following year, when I was able to visit her by taking the train to Staunton and walking to her boarding place.

Every year, Nora went to summer school to improve herself as a teacher. The third year, her neighbors made a special request that she take the school at Darlington Heights in her home community. Here she taught until our marriage in 1910. We saw each other only once a year. In the fall, I spent a week at her home just before I returned to college. Under such conditions many a romance has withered . . . ours lasted.

View from Balcony Rocks, Love, Virginia

Goldie Ann Boggs Stargell

Myra Sandidge Wood

18

Later Schoolteachers

Goldie Ann Boggs Stargell and Myra Sandidge Wood

The mountain schools often employed former pupils who had graduated from the highest grade the school offered or went on to attend "normal" college, which trained students to become teachers. These teachers were mostly young women who were nearly the same age as some of their students. Within a few years, most married and left the teaching profession. These women usually boarded with a family who had children attending the school. Two such teachers were Goldie Stargell and Myra Wood, both originally from West Virginia, who found jobs in Virginia and ended up living in the area where they taught. Goldie actually bought the former schoolhouse near Esmont and converted it into a comfortable home. Myra, whose first teaching job was in Avon, lived just down the road from her former schoolhouse.

GOLDIE STARGELL

Goldie Stargell's former pupils always seemed to have utmost respect for her and said she was the best teacher they had ever had. One of these students, Grace Lank, helped me set up an interview with "Miss Goldie."

Goldie, ninety-three at the time, lived in the old Green Creek schoolhouse where she had started her teaching career in 1931. Walking into the large, open space that doubled as her living/dining room, one could envision children coming into the building and sitting at their desks, ready to start the day. Goldie's life history is as interesting as her career, so read on to learn more about this amazing woman.

Goldie's home, the converted Green Creek Schoolhouse

Goldie Ann Boggs was born on October 30, 1911, to Walter Francis Boggs and Melissa Ann Frame Boggs. They had just moved to Virginia from West Virginia. The family bought a two-thousand acre farm called Willow Hill along the James River in Buckingham County. Goldie remembered the white, two-story frame home had eight rooms and two double-deck porches, the lower one being wrap-around style. Goldie had four brothers, three of whom lived to adulthood, and two sisters, one of whom lived to adulthood.

While Goldie was still small, the Boggs family moved back to Perkins, West Virginia, where they stayed until Goldie was six years old. Her father was a timber man and was often away from home, while her industrious mother ran a general mercantile store and kept boarders who came to work in the nearby oil fields.

From Perkins, they again moved back to Willow Hill, and her older brothers rode horses back and forth between the two locations. The 240-mile trip would take the boys a week to complete, camping or staying in people's barns along the way. One horse, by the name of "Twinkle," was a horse Goldie rode to school in later years. She remembered that the bay gelding with a white blaze and four white feet would get down on his knees to let her mount.

Goldie started school at Mt. Tabor and went through the seventh grade there. She attended eighth grade at Scottsville High

School, but the eleven-mile walk was so far that the decision was made to let her stay with relatives in Goochland to attend the ninth and tenth grades. She finished her last year in high school (eleventh grade) back at Scottsville, riding Twinkle the eleven-mile distance by herself, never missing a day.

Upon graduation, Goldie wanted to attend college to become a nurse, but the cost of the three-year program was more than the family could afford, so she decided on a teaching career, which was a one-year course. She graduated high school on a Friday and began classes at Longwood College the following Monday, studying during the summer semester. She continued through the fall and winter semesters, received her elementary school teaching certificate, and applied for a position. When a teacher asked why she was not completing her last semester, Goldie explained the family's lack of funds. The teacher said she knew a man who helped educate young men and would talk to him about funding a young woman. The man generously agreed, and Goldie returned for the last semester to complete her education in 1930.

Her first teaching position was at Paynes School in Buckingham County, Virginia. Paynes was a one-room school, grades one through seven with thirty students. Her pay was fifty-seven dollars a month. The next year she heard of a job in Green Creek in Albemarle County and taught there during the 1931–32 session. Goldie boarded with the Stargell family who lived just down the road from the schoolhouse.

The Stargells had a son by the name of Herman who took a liking to the young school marm, even though he was dating another girl at the time. By the 1932 school term, however, Goldie and Herman were dating exclusively. Goldie's salary was now at sixty-seven dollars a month, which was good pay back then, considering her room, board, and meals for five days was only two dollars and forty cents. She bought a Model A Ford for two hundred and forty dollars, with a monthly payment of ten dollars, and drove home to Willow Hill on Fridays to spend the weekends with her mother, returning to Green Creek early Monday morning to teach.

While at Green Creek, Goldie taught Grace Thacker and her sister Bertha, who not only were her students but became lifetime friends as well. The girls lived in Bungletown, just a short distance away, walking the mile through the woods to attend school. The girls remembered carrying buckets of water from the spring back to the schoolhouse each day for the children's supply of drinking water.

The Green Creek Schoolhouse at the time Goldie taught there

Green Creek was heated with wood the Stargell family supplied and the county paid for. The large, cast-iron potbellied stove was located at the center of one wall of the classroom. Blackboards also graced this wall, and six tall windows occupied the opposite wall, letting in sunlight. There were oil lamps for dreary days. The students had wooden desks with inkwells and cubbyholes underneath for books. In front of the classroom was the teacher's desk and in the rear, a coat closet. Outside were two outhouses, one for the boys and a two-holer for the girls.

The day began with Goldie ringing the small bell to summon the children inside at nine o'clock. The young children were taught first, with the older ones helping until it was time for their lessons. At ten-thirty, there was a half-hour recess, and lunch was at noon. After the children ate, they would pay dodge ball, seesaw, marbles, and hide-and-seek. There was a fifteen-minute recess at two o'clock to let the children run off excess energy before the school day ended at three. Although teachers had permission to discipline, Goldie said she didn't have to do so very often. "Back then, children had respect for their teacher, and we had the support of the parents," explained Goldie.

The various holidays were all celebrated, especially Christmas, when Goldie planned an "entertainment" with the children participating in a play depicting the birth of Christ. A tree was decorated with strung popcorn and paper chains.

From Green Creek, Goldie went on to teach at Old Dominion School for the 1933–34 term. This school was only five miles away.

I taught for one year before Herman and I decided to get married on July 5, 1935. We got married at the Buckingham County Courthouse. I wore a pale blue dress trimmed in white lace, and Herman was handsome in a suit. Back then, if a woman teacher got married, they wouldn't let her teach for one year after marriage, thinking perhaps she would have a baby in that time. But Herman and I never had children.

I didn't teach from September until Christmas of that year, but another teacher over at Esmont got pregnant, so they called me. We sometimes lived with my mother over at Willow Hill, but when I got a four-year teaching position at Cismont, we lived the first year in Charlottesville. The second year, I boarded with Mrs. Mary Shackleford, and the last two years a man who bought a big estate called Rollaway Hill Farm asked Herman to work there, so we lived in a cottage on the property.

I was then transferred to Alberene School, where I was teaching when someone called to tell us the Green Creek School, which was now closed, was going to be sold. In 1940, Herman and I bought the schoolhouse, and the one-acre lot it sat on, for three hundred and fifty dollars, which included the lawyer's fee. For sixteen years, we lived in it, as is, without putting up any walls.

We got electric in 1949 and indoor plumbing in 1950. In 1956, we added a bedroom and a screened porch. In 1968, we added a kitchen and bath. And in 1993, we enclosed the screened porch and made another bedroom out of it.

Goldie said she always loved living in the country better than the city. The Stargells led an active life, full of hard work but with plenty of time for fun. Their nephew, Roland Leap, remembered coming to stay with his aunt and uncle during the summer months and loving every minute of it.

A typical day for Goldie, while she was still teaching, went something like this.

> I'd get up before five o'clock in the morning to prepare a big breakfast for Herman and myself. Then I'd do the dishes and head out to feed and milk the nine cows we kept besides the other farm animals. After milking, I'd separate the cream then come in to get cleaned up and dressed for work. I'd make lunch for us both before going to work.
>
> Once there, I'd build a fire in the schoolhouse stove to warm the building and then go out and carry in water for washing and drinking. I'd teach all day then come home and gather the chicken eggs and start supper. We'd do the evening milking, and afterwards, I'd clean up the kitchen and do the dishes. After that was over, I'd grade papers and then Herman and I would maybe play cards until ten o'clock before going to bed.

In addition, Goldie helped her husband drive the tractor and put up hay, along with the other farm work. Goldie's nephew Roland had a few words to say about his aunt. "What a woman!"

Goldie retired from teaching in 1972, after forty-one years of service. The Stargells celebrated their fiftieth anniversary before Herman passed away in 1987. On her ninetieth birthday, the family threw Goldie a large party held at Mt. Tabor Baptist Church, where Goldie was an active member. There were many friends in attendance, and every person invited came to honor the lovely lady whose life had touched their own.

At the end of my interview, I asked Goldie how times had changed since she was a teacher. She was quick to point out that in today's academics, teachers do not have the support of parents or the ability to discipline students. She also said that schools do not drill the children in the basics to form long-term learning habits; they just prepare them for required tests, such as SATs and SOLs. She also didn't think that people have as much time as they used to, to enjoy life. "We always had time to visit back and forth, having watermelon-eating contests and hay rides. But I thank the Lord every night for the good life I've had. I've never been hungry or cold and have always had good health."

And we thank the Lord for Miss Goldie, for allowing her to touch so many lives.

MYRA WOOD

Miss Myra Sandidge came to the community of Avon, Virginia, in 1942, fresh from four years at Bluefield College and ready to embark on a teaching career.

Born on May 21, 1913, Myra was the second of eight children born to Phillip and Ollie Sandidge. Myra's family lived just four miles outside of Beckley, West Virginia, in a small hamlet called Harper. Her father worked in the coal mines and also on the railroad, while her mother stayed home and raised the growing family.

Myra and her three brothers and four sisters attended grades one through eight at Harper Elementary School, and she completed grades nine through twelve and graduated in 1931 from the Stratton High School in Beckley. She was eighteen. After high school, Myra did domestic work for seven years to earn money for her college tuition.

Myra explained that about the only two professions open to black women at that time were teaching and nursing. Since she did not have the desire for a career in nursing, she enrolled in Bluefield Teachers College in the fall of 1938 and continued to work while attending classes. While school was in session, Myra lived in the college dormitories, but she went back home to Harper to live with her family during the summer months.

After graduating in the spring of 1942, Myra received a tip from a friend living in the Afton, Virginia, area that a teaching position was available at the Avon School, located next to the Union Baptist Church. She applied for the job, was accepted, and found herself moving to Virginia to begin the fall term. After securing room and board with one of the local families, Myra began teaching as many as fifty students at a time in the one-room schoolhouse at Avon. At the beginning, Myra walked to school, but she began saving her salary, which was between fifty and sixty dollars a month, and later bought a car.

Describing the school itself, Myra said it was sometimes a challenge to get that many children seated inside the weatherboard building. Desks were both individual and two-seaters, with cubbyholes in the bottom for books. The curriculum back then included the basic "3 Rs," as well as history, geography, and spelling. Avon School taught grades one through eight, with different age groups divided into sections. Older children helped the younger ones with their lessons. The teacher's desk was at the front of the classroom. There was a large blackboard and plenty of windows to let in the light, although by that time, the school was equipped with electric lighting.

The Avon School as it looks today

The school term ran from September to May, from nine o'clock in the morning until three o'clock in the afternoon, with noon lunch hour and two short recesses during the day. Myra said the children put on an annual Christmas play, which was held inside the Union Baptist Church. The children also made Valentine's

Day cards, Mother's and Father's Day cards, Easter cards, and Thanksgiving Day cards during the year. In the spring, all the black schools in the district came together in Lovingston, where a May-pole was erected and other May Day activities were planned.

Like so many teachers of that period, Myra had a small hand bell to call the children into the classroom at the beginning of the day. The punishment for any misbehavior was sitting in the corner or staying after school. Back then, discipline inside the classroom was not too much of a problem, since parents disciplined their children at home, teaching them to respect their elders and those in authority. Myra said that repeat offenders were rare; all that was necessary was to send a note home to the parents, and the problem would be taken care of immediately.

Upon completion of the eighth grade at the Avon School, students were then bussed to Lovingston High School to finish the ninth through twelfth grades. At that time, the area was not as heavily populated as it is now, and the bus stopped to pick up students either at their homes or at a central location, such as Anderson's Store. It wasn't until around 1967 or 1968 that the Nelson County schools were consolidated, and the blacks and whites were educated together.

Myra taught at the Avon School from 1942 until 1969, when Hurricane Camille ripped through Nelson County, causing untold devastation. In 1969, she went to Ryan Elementary in Lovingston and taught a total of ten years. She then returned to the Afton area, where she taught for four years at the Rockfish Valley School. She retired in 1973, at the age of sixty.

When she had first come to the Avon School, Myra boarded with several families before finally renting a home near the school. Her father had passed away, and her mother and two nephews made the trip from West Virginia to live with Myra. After her mother passed away, Myra began a courtship with Luther Wood, who was also a member of Union Baptist Church, where she attended. In the spring of 1959, when Myra was forty-six, the couple were married at the church parsonage, and Myra moved into Luther's home, just down the road from Williams Creek.

Luther, who was ten years older than Myra, was employed at

the DuPont plant in Waynesboro. He was sixty-four when he retired. Luther and Myra shared thirty-three years of marriage together before he passed away in 1991. Although she had no natural children, Myra's teaching and her solid Christian values influenced hundreds of young people over the forty-plus years she taught at the different Nelson County Schools.

When asked about her faith, Myra said she was raised in a Christian home and was taken to church while growing in up West Virginia. The family attended Reeds Chapel in their hometown of Harper, and Myra said she gave her life to the Lord at a very early age. Although she wasn't sure if she understood all the fundamentals of being a Christian at first, she "grew into" her faith as she got older and never departed from it.

She remembered Reverend J. W. Stewart was the pastor at Union Baptist Church when she arrived in 1942. The congregation baptized people in Williams Creek then, but now the church has an indoor baptismal.

When they married, the Woods owned a nice piece of land on which they raised some chickens, cows, pigs, and horses. Myra remembered her own family having many of the same animals in

Courtesy of Ted Hughes

Union Baptist Church congregation baptizing members in Williams Creek (c. 1942)

West Virginia. As children, she and her seven siblings had chores they were required to do, and each member contributed to the family's good. These jobs included carrying water to the house, feeding the chickens, milking the cows, getting in firewood, and washing clothes. She commented that in today's society, children are not required to do much work. She noted the discipline is different, too. Many of today's children are raised in single-parent families, and the mother is often too tired after she comes home from work and has to start dinner to deal with problems. Children today are not taught respect for others, and Myra felt it would be harder to be a teacher now than it was when she first started her career.

I asked what the biggest changes she had seen were. Myra commented that the area had grown a lot, with houses where farmland used to be. She thought young people were not as courteous as when she was a girl, and maybe that was because they weren't getting the discipline they needed at home. Another thing that Myra said was changing was the way the world pays for things. Everything is put on credit instead of paying cash, and she felt that credit cards were ruining people, putting them into debt that's hard to get out of. I think we'd have to agree with Myra on all counts, that what people today call "progress," has, in actuality, set our society back a great deal.

Myra Wood was no stranger to trials, but she said she'd had a happy life. She was also a wonderful example to friends, family, and the hundreds of school children she taught during her forty years of service.

19

Teressie Fitzgerald Coffey

White Rock, Virginia

I first met Teressie Coffey in 1984, when she was ninety-six years old. What immediately struck me about her were the spryness in which she got around and the gentle humor I saw mirrored in her eyes. During the next five years, until she died on May 23, 1989, at 101, I was privileged to talk with and visit her many times. To me, she was always "Miss" Teressie, even though she was the beloved wife of Charles Austin Coffey for forty-two years before he died in 1953.

There were subtle things I noticed about her whenever we were together. She always had, like so many of the older mountain women, several safety pins attached to her dress. The pins, mind you, didn't hold anything together; they were there "just in case I need them." Another sweet attribute was the way she held my hand in hers when I was in her presence. I can still feel those cool, soft hands caressing mine as we conversed.

More often than not, we saw each other along the rocky waters of the North Fork of the Tye River where she was born and raised. The Ramsey/Coffey families had always held their reunions at Eli Coffey's log cabin in White Rock, and invariably we'd meet up there.

At one of these meetings, Miss Teressie told me the story of her life, which I published in a 1985 edition of *Backroads*. I am proud to include excerpts of that interview in this book about mountain culture. It is fitting, since Teressie Coffey *was* mountain culture.

She was born in a one-room log cabin with a loft; it was located right across the road from the White Rock Cemetery. She was the next to the youngest of nine children born to Lewis and Mary Anne Fitzgerald. They lived, like so many of the other mountain families, self-sufficiently, raising all they needed in the way of food. They sold any surplus to buy staples, such as coffee, sugar, and shoes. They bartered for what they needed down at the Nash Store, which was run by Mr. Clay Nash, or they'd walk a little farther up the river to deal with Mr. Dabney Hatter.

The post office was inside the Nash Store, and the Fitzgeralds would have to walk there to get the mail. Once deliveries began, a man by the name of Griner carried the mail to their home. Large mail-order items had to be picked up at the train depot at Vesuvius. They had their corn ground into meal at Bill Coffey's gristmill up on Durham's Run until Hercy Coffey built a mill a little closer to where they lived.

Speaking of corn meal, I asked Miss Teressie is she knew how to make ashcakes. She laughed and said her daddy thrived on them, and they always had to keep them on hand for him. "My daddy loved ash cakes best of all, and we had to cook them for him all the time. The way we made them was to take cornmeal, salt, soda, and a little milk and mix them up together to make stiff dough. Then we'd pat out the cakes and put them right on the warm hearth. We'd cover them over with hot coals and let them bake, say, about a half an hour. Then we'd rake the coals off as best we could, dust them off, and eat them." When I asked if they were gritty, Miss Teressie laughed and said, "Lord, yes child, they was as gritty as anything!"

In making homemade lye soap, Teressie said they would take an old metal bucket and punch holes in the bottom and then add a layer of straw. They would put some ashes in on top of the straw and pour water over them. When the water began to drip through, an enamel pan was put under the bucket to catch the lye water. When asked how they knew if the lye was strong enough to make soap, Miss Teressie said they would dip a chicken feather into the liquid; if the lye ate off the individual pieces of the feather, it was ready. When I expressed my fears about what it would do to your skin if it were strong enough to do that to a feather, she quickly reassured me that once the lye was mixed with lard and made into soap, it actually made the skin soft to the touch.

Miss Teressie said that when she was little, she had thick, curly black hair.

Just like if I had a permanent today, that's the way it was all the time back then. We wore calico dresses and feed-sack "under drawers" that Mama made us. We had to wear knit stockings that were made from the wool we'd buy from people who kept sheep. We would card and spin the wool ourselves.

I went to the old White Rock School, and when I entered the first grade, I already knew my ABCs. We had a man teacher with the odd name of Lillian Smith. At recess, we'd

Courtesy of Carl Coffey

play blindman's buff, and it was always such fun. Once, in school, I got an accidental "switching" when some other kids were acting naughty. I was sort of in the middle of where they were sitting and when the switching started, I got a little of it. I never forgot that, and it hurt me on the inside more than it did on the outside.

We'd all go to church and raise our voices to hymns like "Sweet Bye and Bye," "Going Down the Valley," and one called "There's a Land beyond the River That They Call the Sweet Forever."

I stayed home until I was twenty-three years old and then I married Charlie Coffey in 1911. We moved in with my parents from October until March of the following year, then we got

Teressie and Charlie Coffey at their home in White Rock

Courtesy of Carl Coffey

Teressie (seated) with daughters Myrtle and Eula and infant son Woody (who died at the age of four)

our own place up in the holler behind the White Rock Church. Our only neighbors up there were Mr. Joe Fitzgerald and Rob Coffey.

Charlie worked in timber and we raised corn for a living. We had four children born to us, three girls and one little boy who died of pneumonia when he was only four. Funerals were held at the graveyard instead of church, and the body was kept at home for a day or so before the funeral took place. A man by the name of Lampkin Coffey was the carpenter who made most of the wooden coffins for the funerals. They say he made his wife's coffin before she died, and they kept dried apples in it until they needed it.

Miss Teressie admitted that she smoked a corncob pipe. "Been smokin' it since I was five years old. I was too little to even light the match for it, so my mama lit it for me. I had the 'tissic' (asthma), and the doctor told my mama that drawing the warm smoke into my lungs would be good for it. Anyways, it did help me get over it, and I've been smoking ever since."

I asked her daughter, Gladys Taylor, what kind of tobacco her mother smoked and she said, "Oh, it's that old Mickey Twist type that is so strong that I've got to open the windows and go in the other room whenever she starts." When asked how often she smoked her pipe, Miss Teressie said, "Whenever I takes a notion!"

I couldn't help but ask, "Miss Teressie, didn't people tell you that smoking was bad for your health?" A slight smile crept across her face as she replied, "Yes, but they are all dead now." When I got done laughing, the interview drew to a close, but not my memories of the diminutive mountain woman with the corncob pipe named Miss Teressie Fitzgerald Coffey.

Miss Teressie smoking her corncob pipe

20

Riving Wooden Shingles

Hershel Bridge; Stuarts Draft, Virginia

Before the myriad colorful asphalt shingles that grace the roofs of today's homes, there were wooden shingles. The majority of mountain people either knew how to rive (split wood for) shingles themselves or knew someone in the area that was competent in the craft.

The log cabin in Chicken Holler where my husband Billy grew up had a shingle roof, and he tells stories of being able to see the stars at night through the cracks between the shingles or waking up in the morning to find a fine layer of snow covering the quilts on his bed. Amazingly, no one ever complained about the rain coming in. Possibly because the moisture swelled the wood, making a tight fit that water didn't penetrate.

The materials for making wooden shingles were usually within a stone's throw of the roof they would be nailed to. Chestnut wood was the top choice for mountain shingles, or "shakes," as they were sometimes called. Chestnut was also used to build split-rail fences, many of which are still visible along the Blue Ridge Parkway. The wood was used extensively until a blight hit during the 1920s, destroying the abundant chestnut forests surrounding the Blue Ridge.

Over the years, I had often heard many of my older neighbors talk about the way shingles were nailed onto cabin, barn, and outbuilding roofs, but I had never seen an actual demonstration of the craft. One hot August day in 1989, Hershel Bridge set up a shingle riving operation at Pine Spring Camp, where campers could get a firsthand look at how it was done. Hershel was one of the few men who still knew how to split and shave the wooden shingles, and he had cut a crude draw horse, or shaving horse, on which to work. As he worked, he explained the process.

Shingles were made from a straight-grained round of wood, called a bolt, that measured eighteen inches in length and twelve inches in diameter, which was then quartered. From these quarters, four- or five-inch-wide pieces were cut along the grain of the wood using a tool called a froe. A wooden mallet was used to pound the froe into the wood, and the shingles were then pulled off as they split. The edges were straightened with an axe or, as Hershel used that day, a machete. (He had recently acquired one during a mission trip to Haiti.)

After making a draw horse, which is a wooden device that holds the shingles steady while a drawknife smoothes them, Hershel cut the shingles. He said that he had had the round of wood for a long time and was waiting for the opportunity to show the ease with which it could be split.

After a pile of shingles were cut with the froe, they were taken to the draw horse, clamped down with a wooden vise, and shaved smooth by pulling a tool called a drawknife across them. The person making the shingles would sit on the top of the horse while shaving or sit on a round of wood directly behind it.

The finished shingles measured eighteen inches long, four to five inches wide, and a half-inch thick. In 1900, the shingles sold for five dollars per thousand. "Leftovers," such as the shavings and larger trimmed pieces, were used for kindling.

The shingles were put on starting at the bottom, and an inch or more was allowed to hang over the roof to allow rain and snow to run off. They were spaced about a quarter inch apart to allow for expansion. The shingles were nailed onto sheeting boards that went horizontally across the roof rafters. With each successive row, the joints were staggered, so the gap wouldn't fall directly over the one below it. This prevented water from seeping through the joints and penetrating the roof. The shingles were overlapped as each row was laid out up to the top of the roof. There were dif-

Splitting the shingle

Shaving it smooth

Trimming the edges

Teaching the next generation

ferent ways of finishing the ridgeline once the last row of shingles was nailed on.

Pictured are three examples of how the top of the roof could be finished off. The first photo, which was taken of an old building in Kerr's Creek, shows long boards lying horizontally across the ridgeline. The second photo was taken at the Cyrus McCormick Farm in Raphine and shows smaller cut shingles overlapping each other

Building at Kerr's Creek
with a horizontal ridgeline

Cyrus McCormick farm
with an overlapping ridgeline

Building at Humpback Rocks
with a "turkey feather" ridgeline

along the top of the roof. The third photo was taken at the nineteenth-century farm at Humpback Rocks on the Blue Ridge Parkway, and it shows how the last row of shingles was raised up and over the ones on the other side. This type of ridgeline finishing is called a "turkey feather."

Wood shingles are still used on newly constructed homes, but they are now manufactured in plants that use the wood from red cedar. Although they tout the shingles (or cedar shakes, as they are commonly called) as able to repel insects, they require maintenance every so often, and they don't last as long as the chestnut or oak varieties. Hershel said that shingles rived from chestnut could last up to seventy years or more.

An old building with a wooden-shingle roof is now a rare sight. But they are aesthetically beautiful and extremely functional. You could have one . . . if you're willing to put the time into riving your own shingles.

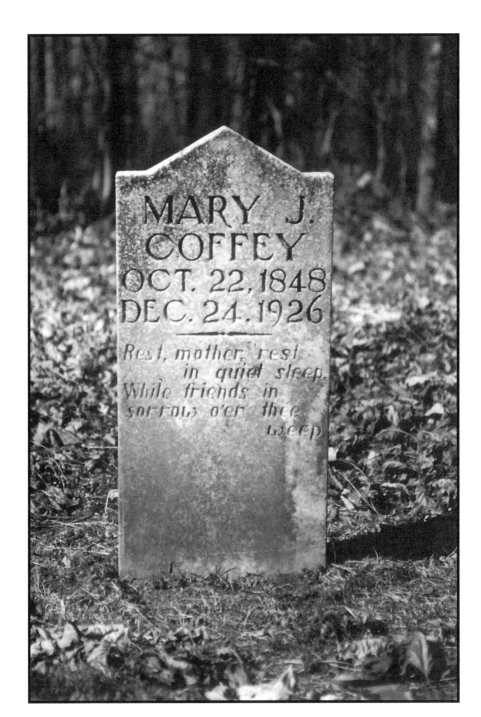

21

Burial Practices

I have always been intrigued with the burial practices here in the mountains. Over the years I've lived in the village of Love, I've been fortunate to hear what the older folks had to say about death and the traditions of early funerals. Unusual rituals of death, many of which are no longer practiced, were once commonplace and strictly adhered to by the family and friends of the deceased.

Perhaps it was the combination of isolation and the fierce independence of these people that made them attend to death on their own terms and in their own homes and churches, instead of turning these sacred rites over to a funeral home. For whatever reason, these burial practices are worth looking at and remembering as a vital part of early mountain heritage.

In our area, the respectful practice of pulling your vehicle to the side of the road while a funeral procession passes by is still common. It does touch the heart to see others, who no doubt have schedules to keep and places to be, show respect and consideration to the grieving families. I am not talking about just the back roads, either. I've witnessed people pulling over on both sides of a double highway to let the procession quietly pass.

One of the most memorable acts of compassion I've ever seen was at the funeral of my good friend and neighbor Boyd Coffey. It was a large procession with cars backed up the mountain for miles. I was at the end of the funeral line, and as I passed the home of

Russell Lowery, I noticed Russell standing in his field out by the road. He was standing erect, with his hat over his heart, as I slowly passed. I cried the rest of the way up to the graveyard at Mountain Top Christian Church. When I commented on this sight to someone who was at the head of the procession, they said that Russell had been standing like that when they passed, as well. I am proud to say that I live in a place where people still take the time to be that respectful.

There are early records showing that hollow logs were once used as makeshift coffins, and that graves were chiseled in stone to protect the body from Indians, who it was feared would desecrate the graves. There were attempts to preserve the deceased by salting the body and piling rocks atop the grave to keep animals away.

Everything that was done was an attempt to show the sacredness of death and lend dignity to the solemn occasion. I believe that with the passing of time, we have lost something valuable in the way we deal with death—the naturalness of it and our willingness to be part of it. The modern-day custom is to hand the entire process over to a funeral director, who then tells us what the proper responses should be before and during the funeral. In years past, people had to rely on their own resources, both in the materials used for burials and for expressing their feelings. No one told them where to sit, when to stand, how to grieve. They acted according to how they felt and expressed their grief in a more natural and personal way.

In our area, there has been a resurgence of people taking control of how they want funerals to be conducted and respecting their loved one's death wishes. In the last few years, many of the mountain people have been brought back home, and the body laid out just as was done a hundred years ago. Also, the custom of hand-digging graves is still in practice.

I asked my husband Billy why they continue to do this, since heavy equipment is available to make the job of digging in rocky ground easier. He had a hard time putting the reason into words. When I asked Butch Allen, I got the same emotional response. They do it as a supreme act of respect for the old mountain ways and the love of their elders who carved a hard living out of the craggy soil. When a half-dozen men gather at the graveyard with picks and shovels and begin meticulously digging the final resting place of an elder, it is the ultimate act of humility and respect.

EARLY DEATH CUSTOMS

When a person died, at the exact time of death, the kitchen or mantle clocks were stopped and covered with a cloth that was not removed until after the funeral. A doctor would be called in to pronounce death and fill out the death certificate. Once word spread through the community of the person's passing, no one worked until the day after the funeral. If a husband died, his widow would wear black mourning clothes for a year after his death. Everyone wore black clothing to the funeral.

BRINGING FOOD TO THE FAMILY

In our area, this common practice is still very much the standard when there is a death. Friends and neighbors start preparing food as soon as they hear that someone has passed away. Some will bring entire meals, or the women of the area will get together to prepare parts of a large meal. One woman may bring a whole ham or several fried chickens, another might fix a pot of green beans, while still another might cook potatoes. Desserts of all types will be brought in. All of this is done so that the grieving family does not have to worry about meal preparation for those who call to pay their respects. In the mountain culture, food still plays a large part of visiting others, and it is considered rude if some type of meal, dessert, or beverage isn't offered to those who call. In church congregations, it is also customary to ask the family of the deceased if they would like a meal to be served after the funeral for family members and those attending the service.

LAYING OUT THE DEAD

Frequently, the deceased had made their own funeral plans ahead of time. They picked out the clothes they wanted to be "laid out" in and gave specific instructions to trusted friends and family members as to whom they wanted to preach at their funerals, who would be pall-bearers, and what type of wood their coffins would be made of. One enthusiastic man had his coffin made years ahead. He used it to store seed corn until the proper time came to use it for its intended purpose. These handmade coffins could be very plain or elaborately carved, depending on the wishes of the family and the time required. Since embalming was not a common practice years ago, time was of the essence. A rag soaked in camphor was used to cover exposed flesh to keep it from becoming discolored. Also, the actual body never went to the funeral home. Instead, someone would be sent to the undertaker's, where a coffin would be purchased and brought back to the home of the one who had died.

Because everyone in the hills and hollers of the Blue Ridge lived relatively close to one another, the burying usually took place within a day or two of the death.

Preparation of the body began as soon as death was assured. The deceased was put on a covered table or bed and then carefully washed and clothed. In the very earliest times, burial shrouds were made, but that particular custom went by the wayside in favor of dressing the person in their clean, everyday clothing. Later still, new, store-bought clothing was used.

Sometimes a rag was tied under the chin and over the head to keep the mouth closed. Coins, such as pennies, were placed on the deceased person's eyes to keep them closed. It has been recorded that a dish of salt placed on the corpse would act as a protective charm.

THE COFFIN

Back then, today's "casket" was called a coffin and was usually made from pine or walnut wood. It was shaped as a six-sided modified hexagon. The deceased was measured and the coffin was made specifically for him. Lampkin Coffey, who lived at Nash in Nelson County, was one of our area's early coffin makers, and many of his handmade boxes were said to contain a glass window for viewing the body. Many remember that he made one for his own mother when she passed away.

When construction was complete, the coffin was lined. For a child, the entire interior would be covered with simple white material. Adults would have white or black material. When it was available and if the family could afford it, lace was sometimes added as an adornment. Pillows were sometimes used to cradle the head. If the person wore eyeglasses while living, they were seldom put on the person laid out in the coffin. Trinkets, photos, and personal jewelry were often put in with the dead.

SITTING UP WITH THE DEAD

Since most deceased remained in the home, the body would be closely watched by different people, day and night, until the time of the funeral. Neighbors brought in food as a gesture of kindness and concern for the grieving family. Because so many of the mountain people were of Scottish-Irish descent, the old-fashioned Irish wake was an expression of respect for the dead and sympathy for the bereaved. Many times, there was music, singing, and general merriment, with remembered good times about the person being buried. The funeral itself was often held in the home, but sometimes the body was transported to the church on the day of the service.

THE GRAVE AND BURIAL

Close friends usually dug the grave. Sometimes there was a person in the community who did it as a local trade. The coffin was hoisted on the shoulders of the six pallbearers, if there were no handles, and carried from the house or the church to the gravesite.

If it was a long distance, a horse-drawn wagon was used to transport the body. In later years, the coffin would be driven to the cemetery in the back of a truck.

An early type of wooden vault, simply called a "pine box," would be lowered into the dug grave first and then the coffin was lowered with ropes into the box. The ropes were pulled out and a wooden top would be placed over the vault before the grave was filled in. The tradition of each person at the service throwing a handful of dirt into the grave before leaving is still practiced in some areas today.

Sometimes, after the grave was filled in and mounded up to shed water, decorative grave houses were built over the top of the mound. Simple tombstones made from flat rocks were erected and carved upon, bearing the person's name and date of death. We have many of these simple markers throughout the mountains where people were buried on their own land or in family graveyards. Many times, a foot marker was also laid at the bottom of the grave. Wooden crosses were also used to mark graves. If the family could afford it at the time of death, or perhaps years later, they would have a "professional" tombstone carved and brought to the gravesite.

I've always wondered why so many of the early cemeteries in wooded or rural areas, untended by a caretaker, usually remain untouched by an abundance of plant growth. Most often, the site is covered with a creeping vine such as periwinkle, honeysuckle, or wild iris that choke out normal green growth. I can only deduce that someone planted these groundcovers at the time of burial, or the abundance of decaying matter and calcium from the bones provided the environment that these particular plants need for growth. Or perhaps it is God's way of preserving the sacred grounds that have been long forgotten by others. Whatever the reason, I always know when I happen upon a family graveyard when I'm out hiking off the beaten path. The telltale "sinking" spots, sheltered by low groundcover, crooked stones sticking out of the earth, will most always be an indication of an abandoned graveyard or burial place.

If you, too, see one of these early gravesites while walking in the woods, take a moment to remember the people of the mountains and their burial traditions of long ago.

Maybelle Campbell and her Jersey cow

22

Grave Digging

Martin Bradley; Tyro, Virginia

I'm not exactly sure when I became acquainted with Martin Bradley. Sometime in the early 1980s, I think, when I sang with a local bluegrass gospel group, and we went to Martin's church for the evening service. For a long time, I didn't know his name. Everyone always referred to him as "the grave digger" or "the mayor." I'd be delivering the *Backroads* newspaper to Cohron's Hardware in Stuarts Draft when the owner, Larry Cohron, would say, "Today we are graced with a visit from the Mayor of Tyro" and point to Martin.

Over the years, his quiet, reverent presence at funeral services eased the pain of a lot of people. I remember being at the funeral service of my dear neighbor, Johnny Coffey. Because I was so close to Johnny, his funeral was very emotional for me. Martin came up and spoke a few gentle words, and his simple gesture really touched my heart because I knew it came right from his own.

He was the one I bought my supply of winter firewood from. And on more than one occasion, he came to my rescue and went far beyond the extra mile the Bible speaks of. But mostly, he was known as the man to call when there was a death in the family.

Martin led a rough and rugged life, but there were changes that softened him and, by his own admission, made him a better man. Sitting at his dining room table for the *Backroads* interview, I began to see why his son Troy looked up to him. And why his petite wife, Inez, said of her husband, "I am really proud of Martin. He's one of the few self-made men in the world today."

Born one of twelve children to Frank and Della Bradley, Martin recalled how tough times were when he was growing up. The family lived in a two-story log home near the bottom of Crabtree Falls, and when the water would get high, they couldn't get to their spring, which was located across the river. He said it would get so cold inside the house that one time, when his daddy brought in the pigs because of bad weather, they froze to death in a corner of the house. More often than not, they would wake up in the morning with a layer of fresh snow covering the quilts because it had blown in under the roof shingles.

When Martin was twelve years old, he and three brothers were sent to live with other families in the area to make it easier on the younger children still at home. He said that he lived with this one for a while and that one for a bit. He finally settled in with his second cousin, Junior Hatter, and his wife Margie for nigh onto fourteen years.

He witnessed the "Flood of '69," which was caused by Hurricane Camille on the night of August 19. The devastation and death caused by the storm was unlike anything anyone had ever seen in Nelson County, Virginia, and it still emotionally affects many of the residents living there, even forty years later. Junior and Margie's house was swept away in the torrent, and Martin helped them build another home after the debris was cleared. After that, he worked on the construction of a new road to replace the one that had been irreparably damaged by the floodwaters.

It was during this time that Martin, in his words, "went on a wild bender" and began to get into all sorts of trouble. He was drinking pretty heavily, and he knew his life was a mess. He was working for a lady named Betty Vaughan when his cousin Junior called with a strange request. A local undertaker wanted someone to dig a grave for a man who had died and was to be buried in the family graveyard above Junior's house. When Martin asked who it was who had died, it turned out to be a man that he used to make moonshine whiskey with. Martin said,

> Me and that old guy was close. We had lived up the holler with some Ramseys and having to dig his grave sort of got to me. In one way, it was a bad thing and in

another, it ended up being a real good thing. Bad because it was hard digging a good friend's grave. Good because I promised the Lord that evening that if He helped me get through doing this tough job, I would never touch another drop of alcohol again. He kept His promise, and I kept mine.

After the job was done, the undertaker called me back and said to come talk to him. He ended up offering me a job, digging graves by hand. Pick and shovel work. I began to dig maybe three or four graves a week. It was backbreaking work. Next thing I know, other funeral homes began calling me. One day, three of us dug five graves in one afternoon, and I knew things were getting out of hand and something else would have to be done. I got a line on a used backhoe up in Harrisonburg, and I bought it. After three and a half years of hand-digging graves, the backhoe was a Godsend. The business kept growing, and I kept buying better equipment to keep up with all the work. I guess you could say it's been a success, but I think my biggest accomplishment this far in life has been giving up the alcohol.

Martin built up his business and made a good name for himself. People trusted his work because they knew he'd stand by it one hundred percent. He was the only person in that occupation to guarantee his work for one year. Because of this, and his willingness to go out whenever he was called, Martin had the exclusive burial rights to certain cemeteries. Monticello, for instance, would only let Martin inside the historic graveyard that belongs to the Thomas Jefferson estate. Many other churches had given him the rights to their church cemeteries because they knew he would do a good job.

I asked if he'd ever been held up because of inclement weather, and he said only once in twenty years of business had he not been able to get to a job. He had been trying to make it over to Ivy in a four-wheel-drive vehicle, but a hard, blowing snow forced him to return home. The funeral had to be postponed for three days until the weather cleared. Except for that one time, Martin said of his work, "There is no rain, there is no snow, and Sundays never come!" He got humorous about his work by saying, "My job is exactly like dying . . . when it's time for you to go, you got to go."

Martin made a lot of good friends over the years, and many of them had requested that he be the one to take care of their grave arrangements. That says a great deal about a man, when he is entrusted with such a delicate matter. Martin kept his word about these things, even though it must have been hard on him at times.

He was a man who strove to do the right thing by the folks he came into contact with. He had always been good to me, and I considered him a friend. I thank him for sharing how he came to be known for this unusual occupation.

The George Washington Coffey home place

23

Handmade Coffins

Burton Chittum; Irish Creek, Virginia

Down the long winding road to Irish Creek, past Nettle Mountain, lives a man by the name of Burton Chittum, who continues the old-time craft of making homemade coffins. Burton, who has worked most of his life as a heavy equipment operator, has worked primarily for the Shenandoah Hardwood Lumber Company in Buena Vista for the last twenty-five years. He is responsible for building logging roads back in the mountains, clearing ground, and cleaning up farmland. According to his wife, Carla, Burton is one of those men who can do just about anything he sets his mind to.

He is mechanically inclined and works easily with any kind of tool, fixing anything that needs repair. He says nobody taught him what he knows; he just picked it up naturally. Currently he is teaching himself to play the banjo, and he hit a few licks on his old Gibson Master Tone during our interview.

When a friend from West Virginia suffered a heart attack, he thought the worst and called Burton with a strange request. He wanted to know if he could build him and old-time coffin, in case he didn't make it. Burton told him, "Well, I've built a little bit of everything in my life, but this is the first time anyone has asked me that. Give me a few days to think about it, and let me see what I can come up with." Burton did think about it and decided to give it a try. He called the man back to ask what type of box he wanted. The man said that in the old Clint Eastwood movie, *Hang 'Em High*, there was a scene where the sheriff was killing the outlaws so fast the undertaker just lined up a row of coffins right on the street. The man said that was just what he wanted . . . a plain wooden box. Thus, Burton began his new career of building homemade coffins.

With no set pattern and just the coffins shown in the Eastwood movie to go by, Burton began designing a pattern in his mind, going to a funeral home to get a few measurements before he started. His friend wanted the coffin made from pure heart cedar without any white streaks in it, so Burton began the laborious task of finding the cedar lumber he needed. Being in the lumber business has helped, since he has access to all different types of wood. Some he cuts and cures himself, and some he buys.

He didn't quite know what to do about a lining for the finished box and the man told him not to worry about it, that he'd just put a quilt inside it when the time came. Until then, the man said he was going to make use of it in his home as a coffee table. Death spared Burton's friend but took his wife's mother, so the homemade coffin he had ordered was used for his mother-in-law's burial. The man called after the funeral to order another and as word of mouth spread, other orders began coming in.

Most of the people who purchase one of Burton's wooden boxes are burying their loved ones in private family cemeteries on their own land, but the coffins can be placed inside a vault and buried in public or church graveyards, as well.

When asked how he knows how large to make each coffin Burton, said he measures the person's height and takes their weight into consideration before he actually starts construction of the box.

Burton uses whatever kind of wood a person wants: cedar, paulownia, and yellow locust are favorites. He has gotten quite adept at putting in linings, as well. One lady ordered a beautiful coffin and wanted a hot pink satin lining. Burton is quick to point out that his unique business is truly a family affair, and his wife and their four children all take part.

From start to finish, it takes Burton about a week and a half to finish a box, working eight hours a day. The process goes something like this. Once the desired wood has been selected, dressing the lumber begins; this takes many hours of sanding to get the

The beautiful workmanship of one of Burton's handmade coffins

smoothest possible finish. Burton uses a tool called a biscuit joiner to pull the wood tightly together so that no seams show. He used to attach wooden battens to keep the lumber from pulling apart, but after someone suggested the joiner, he found that it worked much better.

He then makes sure that all sides of the base are square, getting the angle correct before cutting the top, sides, headboard, and footboard. Once assembled, the glue and other residue are sanded until the boards are perfectly smooth. If there is to be any artwork or the person's name on the lid, that is carved next. Three coats of polyurethane are put on the boards, and then the lining, if any, is added. Finally, he attaches eight wooden handles, three on each side and one at the head and foot, to make it easier to carry.

Although Burton still takes new orders for his homemade coffins, he has been working fourteen hours a day at his regular job at Shenandoah Lumber, so he only works on the boxes when he can. He is very up front in saying that when hunting season comes (September through January), "I won't hit a lick at a snake," and it's best to call to see if he can take another order. He is an avid hunter and, like so many men of the Blue Ridge, enjoys the sport immensely.

Burton is adept at building things other than his line of coffins. He is currently working on a gun cabinet, and he's made beautiful matching table and chair sets, as well as china presses, hope chests, large doll houses, porch swings, butcher blocks, picture frames, and any other type of custom work a person wants. Because, like his coffins, each piece is one-of-a-kind, there is no danger of seeing a duplicate in someone else's home.

Burton Chittum is mostly known, however, for his beautifully crafted wooden burial boxes. Not long ago, he heard from a woman who wanted to order one of his coffins, and Burton told her it would be a while before he could finish it. The woman good-naturedly told him, "Take your time . . . I'm not in any big hurry for it!"

Early mountain people near Love, Virginia

24

Preserving Fruits and Vegetables

Drying, Curing, Burying, Root Cellars, and Canning

The age-old practice of food preservation goes back to the time before refrigeration became available. In my husband's family, as well as most other families in the mountains, electricity did not come into their homes until the middle 1950s. Up until that time, the customs of drying, curing, burying, keeping perishables in a root cellar, and canning were the only ways people had to ensure that they had food year round. Although we now have freezing to add to the list, canning and the other early methods are still very much in use here in the Blue Ridge. I have my older mountain neighbors to thank for showing me how to use these methods, and I, in turn, am passing the traditions on to newcomers and younger folks who want to learn.

I have to admit, there is nothing more satisfying than sitting down to a meal and realizing that everything on the table has been grown, harvested, and preserved by your own hands. My large family will be the first to tell you how obsessive I've become about my pantry. How everything on the shelves is arranged by color and size, so it looks picture perfect. It has gotten to the point that I almost hate to start using what I've canned until after Christmas, so that I don't have to empty the beautifully arranged shelves. And when I *do* start using the vegetables, fruit, and jelly, I keep moving the full jars forward so that there's always a perfect facade in front of all the empty jars. As I said—obsessive!

If you'd like to have the satisfaction of preserving your own food, here is a brief rundown of the different ways you can do it. If you are get-down serious about learning, go to a farm store and purchase a *Ball Blue Book*. It will answer all your questions about canning, freezing, blanching, etc., and has easy instructions and illustrations on how to do it. It's very well worth the price. Happy canning!

DRYING

One of the earliest ways people preserved food was by drying it. Folks here still use this method for a lot of different foods. In the fall, I like to make dried apple rings, which are great for fried pies or just for healthy snacking. They are simple to make and delicious to eat. The older folks dried large numbers of apple rings by spreading them on a sheet which was then put on the tin roof of a chicken house or other outbuilding. The tin roof would heat up from the sun, and both sides of the apples would get an even heating. Even so, it would take several days of being in the sun to complete the drying process. The sheet of apples would be spread once the morning dew had evaporated, then brought inside in the evening before the dew had fallen. When the apples were dry and pliable, they were stored in a pillowcase or a brown paper bag until needed. These early storage containers were the best because they were porous. I made the mistake of placing the apple rings inside a plastic bag, and the bag "sweated," causing the apples to mold.

If you have a woodstove, you can use my easy method. I peel and core as many apples as I want, slicing them into "rings." I put them in a flat container and sprinkle them with a little lemon juice or "Fruit Fresh" powder to keep the flesh nice and white. I had devised a wire frame on which four wooden dowels could be hung, one below the other, by simply coiling the wire into a small loop at six-inch intervals. Attach two wires side by side to a hanger the length of the dowels so that both ends of the dowels will be supported. If you make one, be sure not to wrap the wire too tightly; the dowels need to easily side in and out of the frame. I remove a dowel, slide as many sliced apple rings as I can onto it—leaving a tiny space between each one, then put the dowel back into the frame. I fill all the dowels with the apples and then hang the whole apparatus behind the stove. I leave them there for two or three days (until they feel dry and rubbery) and then place them in a paper sack and store in the pantry. They don't have to be refrigerated.

The wonderful photo (at the start of the chapter) of drying onions was taken over on Coxes Creek at Sadie Lawhorne's house. She pulls her onions up when they are a nice size and hangs them on the side of a log shed. When they are cured, Sadie brings them in for use. Others braid the long green stems and hang the onions from the stems. Many of the older people will only pull their onions up when the signs are right, using an old-fashioned calendar that tells you when the best time to do it is. If you don't do it right, the onions will get mushy and won't keep.

Another staple food for the mountain pioneers was "leather britches." These are green beans that have been strung with a needle and thread onto long strings that are then hung in a vacant corner of the cabin or up in the sleeping loft. The beans are allowed to dry. When needed, the end of the string is cut, the beans pulled off, put into a pan of water with some hog meat, and boiled. I have to say that leather britches are not one of my favorite dishes. They are tough and chewy, but for the early settlers, they staved off hunger during the cold months of winter when there was not much else available.

Most any food can be preserved by drying and then reconstituted in water at the time of cooking. Beans, such as cranberry and limas, are my favorite and taste as good as fresh-picked.

CURING

Many of the mountain people still butcher their own hogs, making everything from sausage and tenderloin to bacon and lard. One of the most popular meats in our area is country ham, which is either salt or sugar cured for a time before it's ready to eat. My first neighbor, Johnny Coffey, had an old wooden salt-curing shed on his property when we moved here. At that time, the shed was abandoned and slowly decaying, but Johnny said he had cured and hung many a ham inside it in years past.

I talked to his brother, Forest, and he explained how he cured his hams. Forest said he takes Morton Sugar Cure, black pepper, and sage, and pats it liberally over the ham. He then takes the meat and puts it on the large table in his curing shed. He repeats this process a second time, adding a little borax to keep the insects off. The meat will age for about six weeks before being hung in a muslin cloth bag that Forest's wife, Eva, makes for that purpose. The meat is then hung in a cool, dry place until it is needed. I remember asking Forest if there was anything else to do after it was completely cured. He replied, "You just take it down and eat it up!"

BURYING

I have heard the old people talk about burying the fruits and vegetables they had harvested, and several explained how they did it. You wouldn't think this method would work, but we tried it last year with some apples and turnips. Sure enough, the food stayed fresh long after the ones we had stored in our pantry had shriveled up. It certainly is an easy method of food preservation. Once again, I've found the old people knew what they were talking about.

Dig a trench in a well-drained patch of ground, about twelve inches deep and as long as you think necessary. Line the pit with straw, leaves, or some other similar material, and place the vegetables on this lining. Cover the vegetables with another layer of straw and enough earth to prevent freezing. On top of the soil, place some boards and another layer of dirt.

This form of storage is good for potatoes, beets, carrots, turnips, parsnips, and cabbage. You can store several varieties of vegetables in one trench for convenience. When you need the vegetables, just remove the boards and push your hand under the dirt, into the straw-lined ditch, and take out what you need. Replace the boards and recover with earth. For cabbage, the trench should be long and narrow. The cabbages are placed in rows with heads down and covered with dirt, the stem ends protruding a bit. This way, they can be easily seen and pulled up one at a time.

ROOT CELLARS

Root cellars were very popular in the Blue Ridge. The back half of the cellar was actually carved into the side of a hill or mountain that bordered the property. The one pictured belongs to Bobby and Katie Henderson of Love, who still use the cellar to store fruits and vegetables. The Hendersons told me that the cellar dates back to 1912 when the former owner, "Buzz" Henderson, hired Mr. Minor Quick to build it. The cellar has a thick wooden door with a screen door behind it so that summer breezes can cool the canned food stored inside. The wooden door is closed in the winter, keeping the frigid air from freezing the food. Most cellars are constructed with dirt floors, which add needed moisture to keep the food fresh and cool. I remember the Henderson's son, Robert, told me that as

The Hendersons' root cellar

a child, he loved going into the root cellar because it was so cool inside. Cellar interiors had bins and shelves constructed along the walls, where different kinds of foodstuffs were kept. Root cellars were a step up from burying, since all one had to do was walk in and select what was wanted.

I remember one sad day when my dear friend Gladys Coffey called to say she needed some help—immediately! When I arrived at her home, Gladys was inside her root cellar with a shovel and several large galvanized washtubs into which she was shoveling a huge mess of broken glass and preserved vegetables. The moisture in her root cellar had rotted the wooden shelves on which the quart Mason jars were stacked. There was a terrible "domino effect" when the top shelf gave way, and the weight of all the filled jars began to collapse the lower shelves. After scooping up all the spoiled food and broken glass, Gladys began to cry. I never understood what a devastating loss this was until I began canning for myself.

CANNING

Of all the preserving methods, my personal favorite is canning. It is the first method I learned after moving to the mountains, and the one I derive the most pleasure from. Friends such as Gladys and Nin Coffey, and Nin's sister-in-law Eva, are the ones I called when I had a question about canning. Their years of combined knowledge always saved me from my own ignorance. Thanks to people like them, the shelves and crocks of my kitchen pantry now hold a storehouse of delicious food that serves us year round. They taught this former city girl how to be a mountain gal, and for that I am eternally grateful. I know that their patience has earned them gold stars in heaven.

When I first moved here, I was amazed to see people sitting in their yards, tending fires under large washtubs filled with quart jars of food. They were canning everything from beets to snap beans and sauerkraut in vast amounts. Up until that time, I thought canned vegetables came straight from the grocery store. These people were canning their own, in a way pretty much foreign to me.

My own mother didn't raise a garden or can food in jars the way these folks did. The mountain people can with a vengeance! I didn't realize until years later that they had done it as a means of survival during the lean years. Somewhere along the way, survival became habit, and even though they now had money to buy what they wanted, the custom continues. Because of the many different canning methods depending on the food being canned, pick up a copy of the *Ball Blue Book* on canning if you want to try it yourself.

Now that I know how to make the food last, my husband and I grow a large garden each year. Our five married children tease us about the work involved in plowing the earth, tilling the soil, planting seeds, fertilizing, picking off bugs, watering, and the endless toil of weeding. We do all this just for the pleasure of raising our own vegetables, fruits, and berries, which we freeze or can after the harvest. Before we preserve any, we get to eat the fresh food, straight from the garden instead of the store. If you've never eaten fresh-picked Silver Queen corn, you are missing one of life's finest pleasures. Believe me, the difference is worth the work. And the work is pure pleasure for those who love the earth and are in awe of the miracles it can produce. Planting a few kernels of corn can feed an entire family. A few dried beans and you've got a meal, especially if some new potatoes are thrown into the pot.

Here in the mountains, summer conversations center on vegetables: how many quarts of beans you canned in a single day; whether the hard-shelled beetles stripped the leaves off your potato vines, or the rabbits nibbled all your lettuce. Groundhogs, deer, and crows can do irreparable damage to the crops you've so carefully tended and are considered "varmints" during growing season.

Johnny Coffey had a macabre ornament in his garden that he swore kept out the crows. He would shoot an offender and hang it upside down by its leg, tied to a balanced stick that was placed on top of a wooden pole. When the wind blew, the breeze would catch the crow's wing and spin it around. The first time he explained what it was for, I had to agree. If I were a crow, that sight would certainly keep *me* out of his garden! Others I know would kill a

Billy and Lynn Coffey's pantry

groundhog and hang it on a fence. This, no doubt, is to make it an example for any other groundhogs with green beans on their mind.

There is a lot that goes along with any kind of food preservation, but for those willing to brave it, the positives far outweigh the negatives. Bon appétit!

The Blue Ridge Mountains

25

Guy Willard Hewitt

Love, Virginia

I met Guy Hewitt and his wife Ora several years before we actually moved here in the summer of 1980. Ora passed away in the spring, just a few months before we arrived. Guy's son Roger and his grandson Norval Dale moved in with him after his wife's death and continued to live in the house long after Guy died in 1989.

Guy was an extremely shy and private man. He kept mostly to himself and didn't bother anyone but gladly welcomed you into his home for a visit or offered to lend a helping hand. With Guy, the phrase "If you need anything, just give a holler" was more than just lip service. It really meant something, and they were words you could count on.

His quiet demeanor and soft voice had an addictive quality, and I'd find myself asking him a million questions just to listen to his "sing-song" voice. I think it was the way he slowly drawled out his words and rolled his eyes that made him so much fun to listen to. The stories he'd tell about growing up here in Love left me mesmerized. He had a unique ability to make things come alive. Some mornings, I'd walk through the woods to visit and end up drinking coffee and listening to him for hours.

I didn't see Guy every day, but just knowing he was down there made me feel secure. Many nights I'd hear the blast of his shotgun down the holler. The next morning when I'd ask him about it, he'd say he heard a noise outside he couldn't identify, so he thought he'd "fire off a few shots" just in case something or someone was on the prowl.

I can still picture him—wearing his faded blue Dickies work clothes and his old ball cap. And where you saw Guy, you saw his old coon dog, Snowball, following close behind. He always kept a few coonhounds, and after dark, he'd turn them loose on the steep ridge behind the camp where I lived. As the cobwebs of sleep slowly filled my head, the last sounds I'd hear before dropping off would be Snowball and Ol' Red making "night music," as Guy called it.

In February 1984, I was preparing to write a special issue of the *Backroads* newspaper that would contain interviews with the older people who had been born and raised in and around the Love area. I asked Guy if I could write his story. Here it is in his own words.

> I was born right up the road a little ways in the old Hewitt home place. The only thing left of it now is the part that my brother Ralph uses for his stable. I was born in 1915 to Mac and Hettie Hewitt, and we lived in that house until I was a teenager. My mother died when I was small and my father remarried, and our family grew to eleven children. We moved across the road over to the Stump place, and I can remember moving all our belongings on road wagons and ground sleds. We lived there a right smart while before moving back to the home place. I stayed with my family right up to the time I got married.
>
> My daddy farmed this mountain and worked in timber for a living. He drove mule and horse teams, hauling logs out of the woods where they were cutting timber. Back then, we owned a lot of this land, but when the Depression came, the bank took about forty acres of it and ended up selling it to the government. They still own the land across the road there to this day. But I can still remember my daddy plowing corn right up there on that mountain where those big pine trees are growing now.
>
> It doesn't seem possible that the land was all cleared and planted here. Yes, I'd go out and call or whistle for my daddy to come home to eat dinner, and I could see him up there in the corn rows plowing with his mules,

"George" and "Lottie." In fact, you could see from the top of the mountain clear down to here because it was all in pasture fields.

Everyone's grandparents helped clear the land with nothing but crosscut saws and single-edged plows. They burnt off huge piles of brush and made the land work for them. When I was a young boy, I raised sheep here. They belonged to my daddy and Mr. Stump, but I tended to 'em. Every night, I had to drive them all in a holding pen so the predators couldn't get to them. I looked after about ninety sheep, all together. I also chopped wood and helped with the farming, too.

My mother put up all our food for the year. Sometimes she'd can as many as four hundred to five hundred jars of vegetables, fruit, apple butter, and meat. We didn't have much money, but we always ate well.

We raised our own hogs, and each year, we'd try and raise a steer. We would end up killing the steer in December so the meat would keep. Back then, it was colder in the winter months than it is now. We would cut off what meat we needed as we went along, and if it started getting too warm, Mama would can the rest. She'd save all the meat skins and leftover butter and boil them in a large kettle and add lye to make homemade soap.

We would go to Waynesboro once or twice a year to get what we needed. We would ride in a wagon filled with extract wood and leave around five in the morning and not get back until way after dark. There was only one bridge between here and there. It was an old one-lane iron bridge located right above Hicks's gas station on the South River. All the rest of the creeks and rivers we had to ford in the wagon.

Once we'd get to town, we would head to Gardener's Extract Company and sell our wood. We had to work for two days to get a big load of extract, and all it would bring us was six dollars. Then we'd go to the store and buy flour, sugar, coffee, and a few clothes. Coming home, we never even lit a lantern. Our eyes were accustomed to the dark real good. Now with all these modern electric lights, people's eyes aren't accustomed to the dark anymore.

I got married to Ora Frances Huffman in 1941. She was over from the Davis Creek area, and my cousin married her sister. They introduced us, and we sort of hit it off right away. I can remember our first date; we rode to Roanoke with another couple in a 1937 Chevy coupe to have dinner and see a show. After we got married we built this same house I live in now.

I asked Guy about the dirt road that ran up the mountain when he was young.

The old road was a terrible thing. It had ruts in it about two feet deep. When it rained, the whole road turned into a muddy mess! Gordon and Henry Everitt had the first car in these parts, and a lot of the time they wouldn't make it up the mountain to their home and would have to get my daddy to pull them home with his mules. In 1951, the state road department decided to pave the road, and it turned out to be a great improvement. Soon afterwards, the electric lines came through, and later, in the 1950s and early '60s, we got telephones up here.

Guy's son Roger remembers hearing kids on the school bus talking about watching a certain program on the television, and he didn't know what in the world they were talking about. Roger said he saw his first television in 1954 at his uncle's house, and from then on, he went over there to watch programs such as *Rin Tin Tin*. "The television had a real small picture and was covered up with 'snow,' but no one seemed to mind it," laughed Roger.

Guy told me about some of the old stores that were located here in Love. There were several businesses. It seems funny to

Guy's grandson Norval Dale Hewitt splitting wood

think that right up the road where Saylor Coffey keeps his cows was once a place where several stores thrived. Of the three stores, which sold general merchandise and groceries, Guy's uncle Hugh Coffey ran one. Another was operated by Guy's granddaddy Joe Coffey. There was also one on the top of the mountain that was owned by Gordon and Henry Everitt. The Everitts also ran the Love post office out of the store, and had a sawmill, grain mill, and a blacksmith's shop. There were a lot more families living here in those days, so Love was a very busy place.

Guy remembered when the Blue Ridge Parkway, which will celebrate its seventy-fifth anniversary in 2010, came through. "Some people weren't too happy about it. They thought it would ruin the land. But it did provide good jobs for a lot of men who up to that time only farmed their land. We walked the eleven miles from Humpback Rocks to Jake Hewitt's place, and it took us a full two years just to level the road down to grade. We worked with cross-cut saws and double-bit axes to clear the land. Yes, things were quite a bit different back then."

One of the stories that Guy told me—one I would always cherish—was about his father, Mack Hewitt, who was helping to build the Blue Ridge Parkway. Guy said his dad was up around Humpback Rocks tending the fires that burned the huge piles of trees that had been cleared for the road. Guy's mother had sent him to where Mack was working to take him his supper. Guy made the ten-mile trip on one of their mules, planning to return home later that night. After he got there, a huge storm came up and began to put the fires out.

As they were sitting there, the men heard a terrible scream. It was what the old people called a "painter," a mountain lion, which were prevalent at that time. As the light from the fires grew dimmer, the screams grew closer. Guy said that they knew the big cat was stalking them. The mule, which was tied to a tree, began to pace and bray, knowing the cat was near. Guy laughed at the memory of him and his father emptying one of the long wooden boxes filled with fire-fighting tools and climbing inside to hide from the mountain lion. "We spent a very uncomfortable night in that Forest Service box. And when we climbed out the next morning, our mule was still tied to the tree but had paced so much, he had worn a deep rut in the ground around the trunk."

Guy remained a close friend and neighbor until he died suddenly in May 1989, while chopping wood. My memories of Guy have never dimmed over the years, and I am thankful for the friendship we shared. I will forever miss his sweet face, gentle laugh, and the wonderful stories that never failed to make me smile.

Owen, Maybelle, and Jimmy Campbell, Montebello, Virginia

26

Horsepower on the Family Farm

Milton Bryant; Montebello, Virginia

The era of mountain farmers working the land with the family workhorse is quickly passing away. For that matter, family farms themselves are gently slipping away before our eyes. Subdivisions and shopping malls have spread outward from downtown main street, taking over the rural land that owners can no longer afford. Here in the mountains, we are lucky to have small family farms that men can still work undisturbed, and life in general is on a simpler scale.

On Fork Mountain alone, there are two men who still keep massive Percherons to do the work that mechanical tractors aren't as well equipped for. Everyone I've talked to says that a well-broken workhorse doesn't tamp the earth down like a tractor, and it can out-maneuver machines on hills and around large rocks without fear of breaking an expensive part.

Mitchael Seaman and his wife, Louise, live on a pristine farm about halfway up Fork Mountain. Mitchael owns an enormous Percheron by the name of Charlie, who he still uses to dig his potatoes in the fall. Charlie is a gentle giant who enjoys a good scratch and a loving pat on the neck. Along with being a working animal, Charlie is clearly a beloved pet.

Another man who keeps a barnyard full of black Percherons is Milton Bryant. Milton and his sweet wife, Doris, live on a farm at the head of Fork Mountain, and everywhere you look, there are horses. Like Mitchael, Milton uses the large animals for just a small amount of farm work, but the enjoyment they both derive from their horses is worth the expense of keeping them.

Milton's family lived farther up the mountain from where he now lives, and he was raised around workhorses. His father, Melvin Bryant, taught his son how to harness and work the Percherons he kept. Melvin never did own a tractor, preferring instead to till the soil with the large, agile animals. In addition to the plowing, disking, harrowing, cutting, and raking hay, Milton's dad used his horses to skid out logs from the forest. Milton remembers his dad's favorite was a Percheron/quarter horse cross by the name of Belle.

Milton has carried on the Bryant family tradition by keeping his own herd of Percherons for use around the farm. A few years back, he purchased a stallion he calls "Frank" from Pennsylvania; he is truly a handsome animal. Milton says that the key to having a well-trained workhorse is to use them as often as possible. Of his own horses, he states, "I need to work them more."

Milton works his garden with a two-horse turn plow, then uses a disk and harrow on the land after it's plowed. Like his father before him, Milton prefers to use the horses because they are easier on the land. A tractor tends to pack down the earth and makes the soil hard to cultivate. The day I took photos, Milton was disking his garden with a horse-drawn disk that Mary Lou Layton left to him before her death.

Another entertaining way Milton puts his horses to use is to hitch them up to an improvised surrey, a farm wagon with school bus seats bolted to the sides, and take all the area children and adults for a ride up and down Fork Mountain Road. He says the longest ride he ever took was with his friend Bill Shuey when they made a fifteen-mile trip in Swoope, where Bill lives, because there's not as much traffic to worry about.

Milton says he starts breaking young horses to work when they are between eighteen months and two years of age. The first thing he does is tie them to a stout post or some equally sturdy place where they can't break loose and slowly begins to introduce them to the harness. He says that each animal has his or her own personality and quirks. Some stand quietly and give little resistance to

Milton preparing to disk his garden

the leather harness on its back. Others tend to buck, kick, and rear up until they get used to it.

The next step is to put them beside a well-broken horse so that they can learn the ropes from a seasoned pro. If you are trying to

Giddup! Disking the earth with horsepower

break two young horses together, Milton says you need one person to lead them and another to drive them. After a while, they get the idea of what you want them to do, and they begin to understand simple voice commands, such as "gee" (go to the right), "haw" (go to the left), "giddup" (go forward), and "whoa" (stop). It takes patience and perseverance, but in a few short years it pays off when you have well-trained horses.

Although Doris does not fool with the horses, she says she likes looking out the window and seeing them, just knowing they are there.

Sadie Lawhorne, Tyro, Virginia

27

Spring Sheep Shearing

Mitchael Seaman; Montebello, Virginia

Mitchael Seaman cannot remember a time in his life when his family didn't raise sheep. As a child, his parents kept the docile animals. As he grew older, he, in turn, continued to raise them. Today, he is the only person in Montebello who raises sheep.

Looking out over their beautiful mountain farm, Mitchael and his wife Louise have an ideal setting for their flock. There is plenty of pasture for all their animals, with the land sweeping upward, high on a ridge behind their stately white farmhouse. The rare quiet is broken only by the occasional tinkle of the bells worn by the Hampshire ewes.

We came to the Seaman farm on Memorial Day weekend, when the spring sheep shearing was taking place. Watching the process for the first time, my husband Billy and I were struck by how fast each animal was shorn of its wool. Eric and Alan Arehart were hired to come in and shear the eighty-nine-head flock. It took them approximately five minutes per sheep to completely strip off the wool. They used a clipper mounted on a tripod that was powered by an electric motor. This modern method is quite different from what Mitchael has seen over the course of his lifetime.

Although he and his father sheared their own sheep, Mitchael's uncle, Wilson Seaman, was one of the best around and was always on hand to help with the annual spring ritual. Back then, he used hand shears, and it took about forty minutes to clip one animal. An improvement was the hand-cranked clipper, which required two people: the shearer and the cranker. Now the shearer could go for as long as the cranker's arms held out. Mitchael laughs at the memory of his uncle singing "Aunt Dinah's Quilting Party" at the top of his lungs, stopping only to yell "Let 'er hum, son" to the one doing the cranking. From there, the clippers went to generator power, then the current electric motors were incorporated.

Others who knew the art of sheep shearing in the Montebello area were Willard Falls and Aubrey Bradley. They were sheep farmers along with Dave and Melvin Bryant and Lester Roberts, all of whom had farms on Fork Mountain. Two men who helped out back then were Clemmer Fitzgerald and Hautie Smith.

The evening we were at the Seaman farm, daughters Bonnie Nedrow and Barbara Brooks and her husband Richard were there to answer questions. The girls have been actively involved in the shearing process for as long as they remember. They have fond memories of being raised in such an idyllic location. Talking with them proves how much farming is still in their blood. Although their brother David was raised on the farm, it is the girls who seem to enjoy the work the most.

When they were children, their grandparents gave each child a spring lamb to raise and take to market the following autumn. Barbara remembers when the animals were sold. The high point was when they got to sign their checks, which were cashed and used for school clothes and supplies for the coming year.

Shearing the sheep was the big spring event in years past, much like hog killing was in the late fall. In the Seaman family, the sheep were driven from their home on Fork Mountain, to Mitchael's mother's home on Spy Run Gap. They all refer to this place as "the farm." Many times, Mitchael would lead on horseback, while other family members walked with the sheep down the dirt road connecting the farms. Bonnie rode drag (the end) on another horse, making sure there were no stragglers.

The family would camp at the old homestead for perhaps a week, rising each morning to go home and do chores, then returning. Both daughters recall the fun of this annual trek. They would ride their Radio Flyer wagons down the quarter-mile path from the old home to the road gate, flying wildly down the hill, bouncing over rocks, and laughing all the way. They enjoyed the old wooden swing that hung off the large sycamore tree by the house. They camped out under the stars on top of the ridge and were able to look across to where Skylark Farm now stands.

Along with all the hard work, Mitchael and Louise saw to it that their three children had plenty of time to play. Many

Mitchael and Louise Seaman, Montebello, Virginia

times, neighboring farmers such as Willard and Vera Falls came to help, bringing their daughters to play with the Seaman kids. Much like threshing time, neighbors lent a hand with no thought of pay. It was a given that when there was work to be done, your neighbors pitched in to help, knowing that you'd be there for them in return.

The sheep, normally docile but skittish animals, know and respond to the sound of their shepherd's voice. Sheep require more care than other barnyard animals because they are virtually helpless when chased or cornered by a predator. Although they are strong and have the ability to stand their ground if the flock bands together, the animals instead give flight when threatened, literally running themselves to death. This makes them easy prey for dogs and coyotes.

Mitchael keeps a ram at his farm but does not let it in with the flock until September when he wants them to breed. Sheep have a five-month gestation period, so ewes bred in September will lamb in February or March, and the lambs will be weaned by the time the grass starts to grow. Twins and even triplets are commonplace, and the ewes are generally good mothers. Every now and then, a ewe will reject a lamb for some reason, and the baby will have to be bottle fed. If the mother's scent is rubbed off a newborn lamb, she will not accept it back. For this reason alone, spring lambs are not handled much. Most of the spring lambs are taken to market at the end of August. Mitchael may keep a few back to replace the older ewes in the flock.

An adult male sheep is called a ram. A young male is a buck and a castrated male, a whether. Females are called ewes (or "yos," as the mountain people say it), and unbred females and babies are called lambs.

There are well over two hundred breeds of sheep in the world, but the Seamans have stuck to basics, raising Suffolk, Hampshire, Dorset, and Cheviot breeds. Mitchael favors the Hampshire because they are stocky, big boned animals; hearty in every way. They have large heads with black and brown faces. The Suffolk is tall and long with pure black faces. Dorsets and Cheviouts have white faces, but the Cheviots have a more delicate build, breed better, and have an easier time lambing.

There have been many changes in wool prices over the years. Back when Mitchael was a boy, his father was paid about forty cents a pound for wool. In the 1970s, the price escalated to one dollar and ten cents per pound. Now, because of a higher-quality imported Australian wool, the American farmer is only getting ten cents a pound. Last year, the Seamans received a paltry sixteen dollars for four hundred pounds of wool. But if wool prices are down, lamb prices have soared, jumping from around thirty dollars an animal to the current eighty or ninety dollars a lamb.

The wool used to be tightly packed into any type of available sack and taken to Klotz Brothers Hardware in Staunton, where it was sold. Later, large plastic bags were given out at the Augusta Co-op Farm Bureau, and the wool was taken there. Nowadays, the huge bags, which will hold over two hundred pounds of sheared wool, have to be taken to the Government Center in Verona, where it is bought by the Woolgrowers Association. Usually between five and eight pounds of wool is sheared off each animal.

Chris Kelly and Richard Brooks stuff shorn wool into bags

Even though all the Seamans are involved in raising lambs for meat production, Bonnie is the only one who enjoys the taste of mutton. When asked what the meat tastes like, noses wrinkle and everyone agrees: "Strong flavored and somewhat on the greasy side." Mutton is best boiled, to remove most of the fat, and then baked in herbs and spices that bring out the best flavor of the meat.

One must be extremely careful when skinning an animal that

the wool does not touch the meat. The lanolin in the wool will taint the meat and make it unfit for consumption. Hands, however, get the benefit of the lanolin when packing the wool; it makes them very soft to the touch. Outdoorsmen and women will agree that pure lanolin on the hands and lips ensure soft skin, no matter how harsh the winter weather.

Billy and I enjoyed our visit, and we finished the day around the Seaman's kitchen table, where Louise served sandwiches, cake, and coffee, along with pleasurable company. The girls recalled many happy memories of growing up on the remote family farm and said how much they still enjoy the familiar work. We teased Barbara's husband Richard that Mitchael's need for an extra hand was why he'd given his daughter's hand in marriage. Richard, not to be outdone, said that he felt sorry for the girls and had married his wife so that she could see what civilization was like. Richard continued his banter by saying, "The farm was so far back in the boonies they had to have *two* pipes to get the sunshine back here!"

Laughter all around. Love all around. At the Seaman farm in Montebello, Virginia.

Vernon and Clora Truslow, Spruce Creek in Wintergreen, Virginia

28

Rural Route Carriers

Tinker Bryant; Bryant, Virginia

Like his father before him, and his grandfather before that, Tinker Bryant was the rural route carrier for Roseland, Virginia until his retirement in 1974 after twenty-five years of service. The three generations of Bryant men combined seventy years of continuous service on nearly the same mail route.

In the spring of 1904, A. G. (Albert Gilmore) Bryant mapped out the first RFD route operating out of the Bryant, Virginia, post office and secured the position of rural letter carrier. He traveled this route daily in an open buggy drawn by horses, Daisy and Tom. He decided not to use the covered mail buggy because they traveled over steep mountain roads, and he feared it might turn over and trap him inside. On the coldest winter days, he put warmed bricks wrapped in blankets on the floor of the buggy to keep his feet warm. Prior to 1904, all residents along the twenty-four mile route had to travel to Bryant to pick up their mail.

Frank George Bryant, A. G.'s son, was the substitute carrier for twenty-one years. When his father retired, Frank was recommended for the permanent position. Frank carried the mail for another twenty-one years until he retired in November 1949. During Frank's time, the Bryant and Roseland routes were consolidated and expanded to a forty-six mile circuit. It started at the Roseland post office, went by Bryant and over Brent's Mountain to the community of Beech Grove, then back across Cub Creek (Ramsey's Mountain), and finally returned to Roseland.

The number of patrons increased from four hundred to twelve hundred. During Frank Bryant's forty-two years of service, roads and mail service improved greatly.

A. G. Bryant with Daisy and Tom

Frank George Bryant, Jr., was born on October 16, 1924. He was the son of Frank, Sr., and Sarah Harvey Bryant. Sadly, Sarah died when Tinker was only four years old, from complications while giving birth to her third child. Five years after Tinker's mother died, his father married Lillian Harvey from Roseland.

The name "Tinker" originated when young Frank kept pestering his older sister Harriet Elizabeth to let him have the Tinker Toys she was playing with. When he began to cry, and she could stand it no more, Harriet threw the wooden toys at her brother, saying, "Take them, you old tinker, you!" The name stuck, and the young Bryant has been Tinker ever since. Bryant was never crazy about his nickname until he found out about a World War Two pilot named Tinker. His plane had crashed in the ocean, and against all odds, he had survived. That, coupled with a baseball player named Tinker completing a brilliant double play, eased the discomfort of having such a moniker.

Tinker said he had been an outdoor kind of person his whole life. By the time he was seven, he had his own garden, learning to work it on his own. "I didn't know how to go about it to start with, but one day my uncle came by and told me my onions would do a lot better if I didn't hill them up to the green tops of the plant." His parents gave him plenty of time to just be a child and play, but he also had regular chores to do. He mowed the spacious lawn around the family home, and he filled up wood boxes for the heating and cooking stoves.

The Bryant home

The Bryant home is a stately two-over-two-style house that Tinker's grandfather built in 1892. Originally, there were two wide central hallways with two large rooms on either side, upstairs and down. More rooms were added over the years, including a kitchen and two rooms to the rear of the house, as well as one bathroom downstairs and two upstairs. Tinker was born in this house in one of the large upstairs bedrooms. The original tract of land that went with the farm when A. G. Bryant owned it was 285 acres. It was later divided in half, and Frank owned 142 acres along with the house. Around 1938, Central Virginia Electric came through, and

Tinker's father had the house wired for electricity. Up until that time, they had used oil lamps. Tinker remembered graduating to Aladdin lamps, "We really thought that was something." The family continued to live in the large home until Frank's death. Then Lillian built a smaller home nearby, where she lived out her life.

The Bryants attended Jonesboro Baptist Church. Tinker remembered that people still came to church in horse-drawn buggies, even though by then most had automobiles. Jonesboro was one of three churches on a circuit with Woodland and Rose Union. One pastor preached at all three churches, with Jonesboro being the main congregation, having services every Sunday morning. Woodland and Rose Union did not have services every week, but when they did, they were held in the afternoon. Starting with Frank's generation, family members were buried in the Jonesboro cemetery. The older generation of Bryants, as well as some Phillipses and Johnsons, had been buried in the family cemetery located on top of a hill just off Shield's Gap Road, a short distance from Tinker's home. A more beautiful and serene spot cannot be found for a final resting place.

Tinker attended the first through fourth grades at Bryant School. He rode there each morning with his father, who passed the school on his way to work. After the fourth grade, Tinker rode the school bus to Fleetwood, which had classes through the eleventh grade. He was seventeen when he graduated from high school. By then, he had been driving for seven years, having learned to back his father's four-cylinder Whippet out of the garage at the early age of ten. He was allowed to drive up and down the dirt road in front of the house until they widened and paved it around 1938. When Tinker was fourteen, he obtained his driving permit by passing written and driving tests, although the examiner recommended, tongue in cheek, that he sit on a pillow so he could see over the steering wheel.

After graduation, Tinker joined the navy. He served two years before returning home and enrolling in Lynchburg College in the fall of 1946. He had a double major of chemistry and physics. His plan was to get a job in some type of laboratory after graduation, but deep in his heart, Tinker longed to have the same rural mail route that his grandfather and father had carried for so many years. He had just started the second semester of his Junior year when he was notified that the mail route he so desperately wanted was available. He had seven days to purchase an automobile and get things in order before starting his new job.

Tinker had been rather a late bloomer in the romance department. "Back then, young people did not pair off with just one person," Tinker said. "We went out as a group, going to different homes for parties where we played games and danced a little." But by the time he got the mail job, Tinker was married to Grace Marshall of Appomattox, whom he had met in college. Before marriage, Grace had been working as a secretary to Dr. Buck at the Lynchburg Training School for the Handicapped. In February 1948, the young couple eloped to South Carolina where they were married. Upon their return, they rented an apartment in Lynchburg. When Tinker got word of the post office job, the Bryants moved back to Tinker's home and lived in a little tenant house at the back of his parent's house.

"It was 1949, and I didn't have any money to my name. I needed a car to carry the mail, so my father drove to an automobile dealership in Lovingston and signed the eighteen-hundred-dollar loan for me to purchase a brand-new Chevy two-door car. On the way home, I remember driving along in my new Chevy, grinning from ear to ear." The mail route Tinker took over was the very same as his father's, with some extensions, making it about a seventy-mile round trip.

Five daughters were born to Tinker and Grace in the years that followed: Rebecca, Louise, Sarah, Patricia, and Frances. During the summer of 1969, when Rebecca was attending James Madison University in Harrisonburg, she was offered an excellent summer job. She recruited her younger sister Sarah to come with her, so on the night of August 19, the two girls were far from their home in Nelson County when Hurricane Camille hit. That night Tinker, Grace, and their three daughters went to bed as usual, never suspecting the water would rise just a few hours later and sweep their house away. Tinker grabbed onto a tree until daylight and was somehow spared, but his wife and daughters all perished in the awful flood. After that time, Tinker and Sarah moved back into the Bryant family home, which had been untouched by Camille.

Three years later, in February 1972, Tinker married Blanche Burkhart, who had worked with his late wife in the medical records department of Lynchburg General Hospital. They had just a few months shy of thirty years together before Blanche passed away. In those wonderful years together, Tinker took tender care of his second wife. She succumbed to Alzheimer's disease on December 3, 2002. Tinker himself underwent open-heart surgery in 1997, but he bounced back remarkably.

When asked what the best part of being a rural route carrier was, Tinker replied, "It was the children." He recalled their names and smiling faces and how they would wait for him to drive in so that they could talk to him. Tinker said there was a handicapped girl who waited for him each day. He started giving her Reese's Peanut Butter Cups, which she called "mailman candy." On the days the weather was bad, he'd leave them inside the mailbox for her.

One of the chief differences Tinker saw in modern times was the busy life people led. "There's no time for sitting down and just talking or listening to someone. Nowadays, people don't even know who their neighbors are. The old people who had time died out, and the children moved away."

Tinker's daughter Becky and her family live in Woodstock. Sarah and her family live in Richmond. At the time of this writing, Tinker had eight grandchildren and one great-granddaughter. One could sense how close he was to his family and the friends who lived nearby. He was delightful to talk with and a pleasure to know. I thank him for having shared his extraordinary life.

Owen Campbell, Montebello, Virginia

29

Sallie Rittenhouse Phillips

Wintergreen, Virginia

On April 10, 1883, just eighteen years after the Civil War ended, a baby daughter was born to Henry and Anna Rittenhouse, who were living at Glenthorne Farm in Wintergreen, Virginia. Henry was the farm's overseer, and he and his wife had two other children born at the farm while he was employed there.

Glenthorne is perched high on a small bluff overlooking the Rockfish River, and the stately brick home was originally part of the Montgomery tract. It has been in the Phillips family since 1914 when John Bailey Phillips purchased the entire farm. The home consists of eight rooms with a huge central hall that spans three floors. The rooms are spacious and furnished with period antiques befitting the gracious living that has touched Glenthorne for more than two hundred years.

Sallie May Rittenhouse was born and raised here and later became John Phillips's wife and the mistress of the beautiful farm where her family had worked. She was one of the few people who can say they lived out most of their life in the same place. The day I interviewed Sallie in April 1983, we sat in the same room where she had been born one hundred years ago. At this time, her daughter and son-in-law, Annie and Ligon Clark, were living with her. They had moved back to Glenthorne to help care for Sallie.

When I took the photo of her in her rocking chair, I noticed a large, handmade basket filled with materials used for knitting, and a

Glenthorne as seen from the front

Glenthorne as seen from the back

sweater that was taking shape. Still active, Sallie looked to be in her early seventies rather than a woman who had reached the milestone of a century. Her beautiful face radiated the warmth and wisdom of those years, and her soft voice recalled the memories of one hundred years of living. In Sallie's own words, I am honored to write her story.

My mother died of tuberculosis when I was just six years old, and I became our family's surrogate mother.

My daddy remarried, but his second wife lived only two years before dying of childbirth complications. So I did the cooking and took care of the other children.

Before Mother died, she taught me to read and write, so by the time I started school, I was way ahead. Our school was located about a mile down the road and we would walk it most of the time. We only went to school three months out of the year back then. I remember my first teacher's name was Eliza Ewing. I stayed at home until I was nineteen years old and then I married John Bailey Phillips. Actually, I was very happy living at home.

At that point in the interview, I asked Sallie why she had married John. She replied, "He just kept asking me!" Looking at early photographs of Sallie, I could see why he persisted. The young woman pictured was indeed a rare beauty.

The couple was married at the Maginnis Hotel in Shipman in 1902. Then they boarded the train for a weeklong honeymoon in Washington, DC. Sallie said they saw the Washington Monument, watched as they made currency at the U. S. Treasury building, and went on a tour of the White House where they saw Teddy Roosevelt's son playing outside the presidential mansion. It was hard to believe that I was sitting here talking to a woman who remembered Teddy Roosevelt.

When the newlyweds returned, they moved to Yancey Mills and set up housekeeping there. After several other small moves, they returned to Glenthorne and bought the entire farm for themselves in 1914. They lived there with Sallie's family, and seven of their twelve children were born here.

The farm's main crops were apples and tobacco. In the early years, three enormous tobacco barns stood on the property. In addition to the barns, the farm had a blacksmith shop, a smokehouse, and a large brick kitchen house with a covered walkway to the main house. There were also ten log cabins that housed all the farmhands. All are gone now, faded into the memory of time.

Sallie recalled more of her early life by telling me about the old-fashioned revival meetings at church.

Young Sallie

Courtesy of Mary Jane Hoffman

We all looked forward to revival time. It was something everyone could enjoy. It was a time for fellowship and reflection on one's life. The women prepared enormous amounts of food, and the meetings lasted all day long. We used to go to the Adial Baptist Church when I was growing up, but when the Rockfish Valley Baptist Church was built, our family started to attend there. We'd ride to church in a horse-drawn surrey until we bought our first car in 1916.

I asked Sallie what kind of car it was and what color. She laughed and said, "The only kind you could get . . . a black Ford!" She recalled that it was so drafty that they heated up bricks to warm their feet in the wintertime. Sallie was a devoted Christian who never strayed from her early faith. "I never drank or smoked in my whole life, and I still read my Bible," stated Sallie.

In 1947, her husband, John, had a severe heart attack and was confined to the house. Undaunted, Sallie, at seventy years of age, took up the art of painting so that she could stay inside with her husband. She had no formal lessons, but beautiful landscapes emerged from under her brushstrokes. With a style reminiscent of

Grandma Moses, Sallie's primitive portraits of the farm and surrounding areas hang decoratively in Glenthorne.

Another of Sallie's talents was writing poetry, which she did in her spare time. When asked how she managed the extras on top of all her other responsibilities, she replied, "I've always been a very determined woman!"

As the interview concluded, I thought how fortunate I was to have met this plucky little woman whose lifespan had seen such big changes. From coal oil lamps to electricity, horse-drawn buggies to cars, and quill and ink to typewriters and then computers. She was witness to it all and remained optimistic about the future. Oh, to have more people willing to live their lives as Sallie Rittenhouse Phillips did . . . determined and Godly.

The following poem, entitled "The King's Artist," was written by Sallie May Rittenhouse Phillips.

The King's Artist

I want to be an artist,
An artist for the King;
To use my talent for Him,
Would only be my aim.

I want to paint a picture,
That might help some wayward soul;
Or be an inspiration,
That might lead him to a goal.

I have in mind a picture,
Of a youth that's setting sail;
Upon a dark and stormy sea,
In a boat that's small and frail.

Then another of anxious loved ones,
Who then an anchor see;
And a compass for to guide them,
In this dark and stormy sea.

I might say we all are artists,
And to each a canvas lent;
And each day we paint and dabble in,
A picture of our life to some extent.

We should be very careful,
That we make the picture plain;
So no one should be in doubt,
That it was intended for the King.

For the picture that we painted,
Ere our journey here is through;
May be another's model,
That they're fashioning after you.

Winter scene at Reed's Gap

30

Logging in Western Virginia

A Brief History, Loggers, Log Scaling

A BRIEF HISTORY

The picture to the left is a 1905 photo of loggers at a camp located in Sherando, Virginia. The photograph was supplied by Bert and Betsy Caul of Covington. Bert's grandfather, George Matheny, was born in 1889; he is the fourth man from the left, top row. At the time the picture was taken, George was sixteen years old.

Throughout the nineteenth century, these hearty mountain men made their living cutting timber and hauling it to the lumber mills. They passed their trade down to sons and grandsons, who continue the occupation. Although the equipment used for logging has changed through the years, the danger is still the same. But the men who log for a living are tough and say they wouldn't consider any other type of work.

Before I retired from publishing the *Backroads* newspaper in December 2006, I wanted to do a special edition dedicated solely to the logging industry. The November 2006 edition, entitled "Full Circle," was the result of talking with the many loggers I was privileged to interview.

Years ago, when I first talked to the late Ralph Coffey of Tyro, he mesmerized me with the story of how, as young children, he, his brother Carl, and his good friend Lester Fitzgerald cut timber with nothing but crude hand tools, hauling the logs from the woods with an ox. As the logging business progressed, the oxen, crosscut saws, and ground sleds were replaced with gasoline-powered chain saws, skidders, and knucklebooms (machines used to load logs onto trucks).

But with any type of progress, there are also setbacks. Due to logging techniques such as clear-cutting and harvesting only the largest and healthiest trees, the land has suffered many ill effects, such as soil erosion and an excess of unwanted "scrub" timber, which could flourish once the old-growth trees were taken. Over time, the very practices that provided top lumber for building and a good living for timber men have taken their toll on the earth.

The last person I interviewed was a young man by the name of Ethan Childs, who is practicing the old concept of restorative forestry. He is a student at Healing Harvest Forest Foundation, which promotes the slow comeback of healthy forests by cutting down "trash" trees and insuring the growth of more valuable timber. The foundation is again using large animals— horses, oxen—to log out the trees, knowing the low impact to the forest floor will only add to its healing. Ethan has made a fulltime commitment to restorative forestry with his team of Suffolk punch horses. His first job is to harvest enough timber on a family tract of land to build a home of his own and supplement his income.

It is my wish to preserve how the logging industry has evolved through the centuries and has finally come "full circle" in the mountains of western Virginia. This chapter is dedicated to all loggers, both past and present, as a special tribute to these rugged, free spirited men who have made their living in the woods and to the wives who have supported and stood by them throughout their often-dangerous profession.

LOGGERS

*John Henry Bradley, 1889–1962**

John Henry Bradley was born June 1889 on Fork Mountain in Montebello, Virginia. One of ten children born to James Alexander Bradley and Martha Ann Painter Bradley, he helped his father farm when a youngster. His father gave land for a school at Fork Mountain, where John attended. At approximately seventeen years of age, he began

John Henry Bradley (c. 1907)

Courtesy of Lyle Bradley

to work as a timber cutter and logger, furnishing timber to local sawmills.

In 1907, he attended the World's Fair held in Jamestown, Virginia. While there, he saw demonstrated a "skidder" that he believed would work well for logging in the mountains. Later that year, he married Pearl Fauber and they had ten children. After he married, he purchased a store in Montebello from his uncle, Johnny Painter. I don't know what year he bought the store, but Johnny left for Idaho in 1913, so I assume it was purchased at this time. My mother operated the store, while my father continued logging and cutting timber.

At a later date, John obtained a skidder like the one he had first seen at the World's Fair. This was the first piece of mechanized logging equipment ever seen in the mountains. It was a converted Ford tractor. On the rear, where the wheels would normally be, was a huge spool or drum that held 1,400 feet of three-quarter or

---

*By Lyle Bradley of Vesuvius, Virginia. Portions of this story came from the book *Wild Catting on the Mountain,* by Benjamin F. G. Kline, Jr., and Thomas Tabor, III. Used with permission.

one-inch steel cable. This cable weighed one pound per foot. The
tractor was mounted on a half-inch solid steel sled.

When used for logging, the skidder was anchored by cable to
a large tree stump. The cable unwound from the spool from under
the front of the skidder, pulled by a horse. An extension cable of
four hundred feet was sometimes used when a greater distance
was required. The cable was then attached to a tree that had been
cut down with limbs removed. The tree was then pulled to the
vicinity of the skidder, which was called a landing. At the landing, the tree was cut into logs for transporting to the sawmill.
The pulling power of the skidder was such that it would break
the steel cable if the tree that it was pulling became lodged or
stuck in a rock ledge or some other immovable object. For this
reason, it was necessary to use a flagman to warn the skidder
operator if the tree became stuck or lodged. Splicing a broken
cable required thirty to forty minutes, so a flagman was essential
to the operation. A block and pulley was sometimes used to avoid
obstacles.

The South River Lumber Company in Cornwall, Virginia

The South River Lumber Company was incorporated under the
laws of Virginia on March 27, 1916. Initial value of stock was one
hundred thousand dollars, held by William Whitmer and Sons.

They had moved this operation to Virginia from Pennsylvania, as no significant timberland remained there.

The logging railroad started at the sawmill in Cornwall. The railroad followed Irish Creek eastward until reaching the settlement of Irish Creek, then, by using three switchbacks, climbed to the summit of Painter Mountain. From there, branches traveled in all directions. The railroad was a forty-two-inch gauge for a distance of fifty miles of track.

Trouble began early. The railroad grading crews were Pennsylvania men experienced in working sandstone and shale that could easily be moved by the use of inexpensive black powder and hand tools. Virginia's granite was quite different. After several miles of grading, the contractor went to the company and asked to be relieved of the contract before going broke. The use of black powder proved ineffective for blasting granite, and the necessary dynamite was far more expensive. The erection of eight bridges needed to cross Irish Creek between Cornwall and Nettle Creek also increased construction costs alarmingly.

Eventually, these difficulties were overcome, and by around 1920, the railroad was in operation. There were fifty miles of track, and before the operation ceased, over one hundred million board feet of timber had been hauled off the mountain bound for Cornwall. My father, John Henry Bradley, had contracted with the South River Lumber Company in the early twenties to cut and log to railroad landings. I would reckon that most of those one hundred million board feet of timber had been cut and logged to the landings by my father and his skidder.

Some of the men who were engaged with my father in this large logging operation were brothers Ralph and William Paul Hite and brothers Turner and Frank Humphreys, with Frank being my favorite. Frank's horse was used to pull the cable. Others were Earl Ramsey and son, Minor; Johnny Campbell; Ambrose Cash; Emory "Snoot" Bradley; brothers Wymer and Weldon Smith; father and son, Howard and Willie Mays; my three brothers, Herman, Wilson, and Lambert Bradley; and Taylor Whitesell, who was the log scaler and may have been employed by the South River Lumber Company. I'm sure there were many more, but memory dims with age. It was said the skidder replaced seventeen horse teams that were being used when the skidder came on the scene.

After the closing of the South River Mill, my father contracted with the McKinley Veneer Log Company to cut and log veneer timber in Tidewater, Virginia. He took the skidder and some timber cutters to the West Point area. Minor Ramsey told me later that it was the first time he had ever used a nine-foot crosscut saw, which was required to cut the huge poplar trees.

I heard this story told about brothers Frank and Turner Humphreys. On this day, they were working as tong-hookers for the loader. The load man yelled down, "Hook me a big one." Frank told Turner to hook the tong into a big chestnut stump that was in the log pile. The load man tried everything he knew. First, the regular way, until the loader lifted off the rail on the uphill side. Nothing moved. Then he laid the boom down level and tried again. This failed. He then turned the boom uphill and double-horsed the line. Failure again. Turning the loader, he slowed the engine and climbing out of the cab, he hollered to the brothers, "All right . . . hook me one just a mite bit smaller."

Here are some things I remember my daddy saying: "The only work that's not honorable is dishonest work." And when asked if a certain person worked for him, he would reply, "No, they work for themselves; I'm just the person that sees they get paid for their work."

Once, while in the Tidewater area, my father was asked by a merchant why he preferred to hire mountain people rather than the locals there. His reply: "Well, I reckon local people might be all right, but with mountain people, you just tell them what you want done, then get out of their way!"

Ralph and Jeff Coffey; North Fork Tye River, Virginia

In December 1992, I published a special edition of the *Backroads* newspaper, which paid tribute to modern-day pioneers; the men who continue to preserve the old-time trades, such as saw milling, building hand-hewn log cabins, and logging. At that time, I was using all three trades to start my own cabin here in Love, Virginia. I interviewed all the men who had a part in that exciting project. The loggers I talked to were a father-and-son team by

Jeff amd Ralph Coffey cutting down a huge red oak tree on Lynn Coffey's property

the name of Ralph and Jeff Coffey, who lived on the North Fork of the Tye River in Nelson County.

When I interviewed Ralph, I was amazed by the story he told about doing a man's work while he was still a child. Starting out with only basic hand tools and an ox, he forged a career in logging that spanned his lifetime. Ralph lost his fight with cancer at fifty-three and passed away on June 10, 1996. This is his story.

Ralph's father, Patrick Coffey, was a logger in the White Rock area. That was back in the days when the men didn't haul the logs to a mill; the mill came to where the timber was located. Pat owned one of the old sawmills, run by a wood-powered steam engine that was situated on a large wagon with metal wheels. Ralph recalled that this portable sawmill had to be hauled to the lumber site by a six-horse team. The mill was set up on the property until all the trees were cut, then moved back to its original location at the Coffey family home along the North Fork.

Ralph Coffey's family. From left to right: oldest sister Charlene, youngest sister Elda, Ralph, brother Carl, Quincey (his mother)

Pat ran the mill until his health failed; then it was sold, along with his truck, to help pay the taxes on his land. Pat died suddenly of a heart attack in 1948, leaving his wife Quincey and four children to make a living as best they could. Ralph was six at the time and his brother, Carl, was eight. The eldest daughter, Charlene, went to live with relatives in West Virginia, and the youngest girl stayed home.

Even at their young age, Ralph and Carl learned more about logging from helping neighbors Boston and Tommy Taylor. The boys continued cutting firewood in the summer months for the family's use, and at the ripe old ages of eight and ten, the brothers combined forces with good friend Lester Fitzgerald, also ten, and went into the logging business. Lester had raised a gentle, white-faced Hereford ox named Mike, and the Coffey brothers had their family land and their daddy's logging equipment.

Working with crosscut saws to
fell the trees and using Mike to
haul the timber out of the woods,
the children rolled the logs up
homemade skid poles and onto a
hired truck. Ralph told me that
some of the men who hauled for
them over the years were Walton
Bryant, Roundy Ramsey, and
Perry Strickland of Tyro. The logs
would then be taken to the railroad for shipping or to the mill
run by Bland Lawhorne.

Lester's ox Mike with J. D. Fitzgerald
and Joyce Latimir aboard

The boys worked well together
and made enough money for
school clothes, shoes, and food for
their families. In the fall, the
entire family worked in the apple orchards, but the boys continued
their logging activities after school and on weekends. Ralph said
he grew up working hard because it was all he ever knew, and it
became a continuous way of life.

In later years, the boys saved their money and bought a horse
team, which was a little faster than Mike the ox. In the middle
1950s, they moved up to a 1940 John Deere crawler tractor. As
soon as Carl was old enough to get a driver's license, they bought
a 1948 Chevy three-quarter-ton truck to haul the logs. Ralph said
he was fourteen or fifteen before he ever went for a ride to the city
of Lynchburg. The boys continued to better their equipment, trad-
ing the John Deere for several Caterpillar crawlers and a log skidder. The old Chevy was updated to a newer GMC truck.

In 1960, the two Coffey brothers decided to go to Fairfax on a
summer construction job that a friend named Arnie Coffey got
them. Ralph said, "We would work there during the week and
come home on the weekends to make sure everything was okay
there and to do more logging. I always came home in the fall to
take care of my mother and my sister and to tend the horses that
had to be grain fed in the winter months."

The Coffeys worked the Fairfax construction job for two summers, but the third summer, Carl went into the military and Ralph came on home to stay. When Carl returned from service, he decided to settle in Fairfax, where he started his own successful business and lived for many years. After retirement, Carl moved back to Nelson County and is now living on a beautiful farm in Massies Mill.

In 1962, Ralph got a job at Fleming Foods working the second shift so he could still log in the morning hours. He married Janet Zirkle in 1965, and the couple had two children: a daughter, Susan, and a son, Jeff.

Ralph said that from the time Jeff was big enough to ride on a tractor, he was either on Ralph's knee or by his side. "He'd come in from school, and even though he wasn't big enough to cut or hook up the timber, he had learned to drive the tractor and that's where he started. At that time, I was driving a truck for Fleming, and I'd take Jeff with me as often as I could."

Jeff grew into the logging trade. Although he has done other types of work, such as construction, and has a college degree as a diesel mechanic, he has always come back to logging. He loves the work as much as his daddy did and continues to be drawn to it. When I interviewed him, he said that there is nothing quite like working in the outdoors, being your own boss, and not having to punch a time card, even though most times he works more than a forty-hour week. He said he can get up in the morning and do what he wants to do. No two days are ever the same, and he gets to see new places and new people on each job.

Over the years, Jeff's skills as a mechanic came in very handy; he could repair all the heavy equipment kept for their logging business. Ralph was quick to point out his son's other skills, such as construction work, clearing land, operating a backhoe, digging basements, and putting in septic systems. Ralph said that no one had taught Jeff to do these things, "He just picked them up on his own." It was obvious the father was very proud of his son.

When asked what the most dangerous part of the job was, Ralph said, "It's *all* dangerous; from driving the equipment and using saws to loading and unloading the trucks and working in the timber. Cutting trees and skidding them out in a steep, bad place is the most treacherous, but that's where you find the big timber. We've been real lucky that neither of us has ever been seriously hurt. But I've known a lot of men who have gotten hurt real bad or lost their lives logging."

In 1992, Ralph said that the most valuable timber on the market was red and white oak. He remembered years ago when a load of oak logs might bring thirty to fifty dollars. In the '90s, that same load of timber could bring anywhere from five hundred to five thousand dollars.

He said timber was being cut faster because the modern equipment could get it out of the woods more quickly and easily. But it was being cut faster than the trees could grow back, forcing loggers to go deeper into the rough places to find large-growth trees. Ralph said that all the easy timber had been cut.

A second growth of pine can be recut in about twenty to thirty years, if conditions are right. Years ago, it took about a week to get out a thousand board feet of lumber. Now, loggers can cut about twenty-five thousand board feet in three days.

The Coffeys have cut timber all around the state of Virginia and, locally, in the areas of White Rock, Montebello, Tyro, Love, Davis Creek, Piney River, Rockfish, Brent's Mountain, and Buena Vista. They used to do all the logging themselves, but around 1989, they had more work than they could handle, so they hired two good men to work with them, David Wilson and Hank Carr.

Traditionally, the winter months are a logger's slack time, and when bad weather arrives they switch off to other jobs, like repairing their equipment. A lot of things have changed since the early days of logging. From jay grabs and trace chains to skidders and knuckleboom loaders, it's a whole new ballgame. But the work is the same, and Ralph Coffey summed up the interview by saying:

> I'll always be a logger. It gets in your blood and you can't get away from it. It's not like anything else you've ever done. You are more content working for yourself, even if you have to work harder. You've got to make money to live, but if you are doing something you love, you'll work harder at it. We worked all the time and

always have. I guess that's where Jeff gets it from . . . we just growed up to it.

Dale Allen and Don Taylor; Stuarts Draft, Virginia

Dale Allen and Don Taylor have worked as partners in the logging business for more than thirty years. In their early sixties at the time of this interview, they continue to cut timber together. They have been friends since childhood and later became brothers-in-law. Dale learned the logging trade from his father, Dennis Allen. Dale's grandfather, Eugene "Hoot" Allen, was also a logger and he

Don Taylor (left) and Dale Allen

used the money he earned from cutting timber to supplement his farming income. On and off, Dale and Don have worked with different men who cut timber, but for the most part they have worked together. They say at some point they'd like to retire, but as everyone knows, once logging is in your blood, it's hard to quit.

Dale said he began logging with his father when he was about sixteen years old, but before that, he remembers going with his father to cut dead-standing chestnut timber in the mountains at Pryor's Camp, were the present Wintergreen Ski Resort is located. The men said that the sawmills in our area quit buying chestnut wood around 1958. Back then, the mills paid around sixteen dollars a cord, which was a pretty good price. As a young boy, Don tagged along with Ray Everitt and Bill Sensabaugh, learning the trade at an early age.

Starting off, the men worked with whatever logging tools Dennis Allen had accumulated. This included a strawberry roan gelding by the name of "Prince," a McCullough chain saw, and a 1947 Ford truck that they loaded by hand using skid poles and cant hooks. Don was in charge of skidding the logs out with Prince, since Dale admitted that "horses just were never my cup of tea." As the years progressed, the men bought more mechanized equipment, starting with an Allis Chalmers front-end loader in 1965, on up to modern-day skidders and knuckleboom loaders. They remember Menno Kinsinger, who ran a sawmill in Stuarts Draft, as having the first skidder back in the 1960s.

Dale served in the army and was in Germany for a few years before coming home at twenty-two. While Dale was serving in the military, Don continued working with Dennis. He also worked for about eleven years with his good friend Everett Allen.

Over the years, the men logged for a lot of different lumber companies and saw mills, including Smith in North Garden, Fitzgerald Lumber in Fairfield, and several outfits in Buena Vista. The South River Lumber Company in Cornwall had the timber rights in and around the Montebello area, including Norval's Flats and Crabtree Meadows. These companies would get a logging contract on a certain tract of land and then hire loggers like Dale and Don to cut the timber. While they mostly worked these areas

Dragging out a log with a skidder   Loading logs onto a truck with a knuckleboom

close to home, they once took a job in Roanoke, which was the farthest they ever went.

When asked what the most difficult job they ever did was, both men were quick to say it was a tract of land at Brown's Cove near Whitehall. "It was real steep mountain land that joined the Skyline Drive near Route 33."

When asked what the *best* part of their job was, Dale made us all laugh with the comment, "When you get your check!" Traditionally, there is a fifty-fifty arrangement between the landowner and the loggers, but if there is an abundance of good veneer lumber, the scale is tipped in the landowner's favor. Although much of the timber has already been harvested in this area, Dale and Don both agree there is still a lot of good wood left on private land.

They remember lumber camps that were built close to the dinky railroad lines that wound their way through the mountains. The mills built these shantytowns to house workers and their families on logging locations. When the job was finished, each shanty was loaded on a railroad car and hauled to the next location. Dale's grandparents, Eugene and Ethel Allen, lived in one of the company houses at Norval's Flats when Dennis was just a small boy. Dale said there were also a lot of shanties set up at Pryor's Camp, where Wintergreen Resort was built. Back then, a man by the name of Maddox owned all that land, which was then known as the "Big Survey."

In the mountains, oak is probably the most valuable timber, with poplar and locust coming in next. In the valley, white oak and walnut have the most value. Pine is plentiful everywhere but does not bring as much money as the hardwoods.

Don and Dale, along with their current helper, Jimmy Shorter, usually cut and haul out two loads of logs per day. In years past, they had also employed "Shorty" Phillips, Butch Allen, and Dale's son, Jerry Dale, who is a full-time state trooper but still cuts timber on the side. As stated before, if a man is exposed to logging at an early age, it gets into his blood.

When asked if logging has provided them with a good living, both Don and Dale agree that they love what they do. Along with the hard physical work, the job is also very flexible, allowing the men to take most of the winter months off to work on equipment and participate in a logger's favorite pastime: bear hunting! Although neither is wealthy, Dale says that each has a roof over his head, and Don adds that they pretty much can buy whatever they want. Plus, they love the freedom of being in the woods and not having to punch a time clock or work for anyone else.

Both men have been blessed that neither of them has ever been seriously hurt while logging, something that a lot of others in the profession cannot say. But even with all the risks, Dale Allen and Don Taylor wouldn't want to do anything else and are happy to have had a lifetime career of cutting timber.

Ethan Childs; Ivy, Virginia

This story is told almost entirely in Ethan's own words.

I grew up on a tree farm in a log cabin . . . my dad and his neighbor used horses to pull out poplar logs that were cut in our woods and drug to our home site. My parents and my grandfathers actually built our house together. I was always fascinated by the conventional logging process with all the droning machinery, but I couldn't help but notice how much less of an impact on the land there was when horses were used. Years later, this same thought came back to me, influencing my decision to become a biological woodsman.

As children, my dad encouraged me and my two sisters to ride horses, and I did my share when I was younger. But by the time my sisters were in middle and high school and very involved in the pony club, I was not as involved with the horses anymore. It wasn't until I met my wife, Tyler, who is a horse trainer, that I started to ride again.

I met Jason Rutledge and Chad Vogel two years ago, when my wife, Tyler, and I were married. I was taking a forestry class, and one of the students invited the whole class to a directional felling and horse-logging workshop that Jason was hosting at the student's farm in Madison County called Gibson Hollow. It was there I first learned about "worst-first" single tree selection.

Meeting these men was so inspirational that a few weeks later I called and asked if I could start an apprenticeship. A usual apprenticeship takes about six weeks if completed all at one time. For me, it took longer because I was working at the time. I run a fulltime landscape business called Woodland Scapes, so I had to do it on a part-time basis, going up to Fauquier County where they were at, sometimes one or two days a week and then driving back to my home in Ivy. It took me between six and eight months to complete my apprenticeship. Both men mentored me through my apprenticeship, with Chad being closer to my own age and Jason being the senior leader.

During this apprenticeship, I learned the few basic principals that Healing Harvest Forest Foundation is based on: never taking more than a third of canopy space, that third consisting of the worst value of the trees that are there. These are determined by how many defects are apparent, such as leaning, frost cracks, or if the tree's crown is damaged. Also, they look at removing species of lower economic value such as hickory or gum. By removing these lesser species, it gives the healthy trees less competition of light and nourishment, more space for the canopy to grow out and maximize their potential for growth.

What we do is the exact opposite of high grading, which is one of the most common selective cuts that loggers do these days. They go in and pick the best timber, cut it, and haul it to the sawmills, leaving a residual of unhealthy trees in the forest. By cutting the best timber, they are taking away the valuable seed stock, that valuable reproductive tree, and removing its DNA from the forest.

If you look at it like a stock portfolio, you wouldn't want to sell your best stocks. You'd want to hold onto them because they have long-term profit potential. On the other hand, the stock that's not really going anywhere, that never is going to be worth that much, that's the one you want to remove from your portfolio. I'm comparing stocks to timber species; the valuable trees such as red oak being the best stock and, say, gum as being a lesser stock value.

Healing Harvest Forest Foundation strives to develop a long-term relationship with landowners with the understanding there will be a successive harvest, and come back in fifteen to twenty-five years and do the same thing again, taking out the lesser trees and leaving the best timber, once again only taking a third of the worst of what's left.

As a prime example, Pioneer Forest in Missouri has been operating on the "worst-first" single-tree-selection principle since the 1920s. Clint Trammel, who is the current forest manager says the trees they are taking out, which are the worst of what is growing in that forest now, is better than what they were leaving on the first harvest.

When I asked Ethan about the value to the landowner, as well as the logger doing the "worst-first" cutting, he said, "You just have to make the most of it. Some timber can be sold as firewood. Others can be sold as saw logs, which makes the most money. This type of lumber is being used for cabinetry, building homes, and fine furniture. Veneer lumber is the best, of course, but we don't cut that unless we're clear cutting an area. By leaving these veneer logs, encouraging them to grow more, landowners managing their forest lands for long-term investment are making the wisest choice."

In September 2006, Ethan, Tyler, and their son Linden moved to King William, where Ethan planned to begin the first phase toward becoming a full-time biological woodsman. Using his own land as his first woodland job, he was to clear cut twenty-five acres of an eighty-acre family farm. There he would build a home and use the surrounding open land for pasture for his three Suffolk punch workhorses, as well as Tyler's show horse.

Ethan aboard his Suffolk punch horse team

On those twenty-five acres, he planned to leave a stand of three to five trees per acre for shade. The remaining acres of forest would be managed on the "worst-first" single-tree-selection principle. A neighbor who owns an adjoining tract of land also showed interest in having her property logged by Ethan, which would have given him a nice employment opportunity close to home. Unfortunately, I lost touch with Ethan after his move, so I have no idea whether he was able to achieve his goals.

When asked what the best part of being a biological woodsman is, Ethan, like all the other loggers interviewed, said, "Being outdoors and working with my horses; doing something that my parents and grandparents did so many years ago. Looking at early photographs of them, seeing them so young and vibrant, has inspired me to see myself fitting into the same mindset in my own lifetime."

LOG SCALING

Butch Allen; Stuarts Draft, Virginia

In the logging industry, there are people who buy saw logs from the men bringing them in by the truckloads. These people are called log scalers, and it is their job to individually price each piece, tell the logger how many board feet he has in the load, and how much cash the load will bring.

Lynn "Butch" Allen retired in February of 2009 from Fitzgerald Lumber Company in Raphine, Virginia, where he had worked as a log scaler for twenty-eight years. He's been involved in every facet of the logging trade for most of his life, like his brother Dale. He, too, can remember being five or six years old and going along with his father, Dennis Allen, who was logging extract wood up at Pryor's Camp. He said that back then, his dad used a horse to skid the trees out of the woods and loaded them onto his truck with cant hooks. Dennis also had a Frick sawmill on his farm with which he cut lumber. Butch remembers cutting maybe ten to fifteen truckloads of logs and bringing them back home, where they would spend time turning the logs into lumber.

When Butch graduated from high school, he served two years in the military, from September 1966 until September 1968, before coming home, buying his first truck, and going into the logging business himself. At first, he worked with his dad, his brother Dale, and good friend Don Taylor.

As time went by, he married and had three children. It was hard to make a living cutting pulpwood, so Butch decided to get a factory job that paid better wages. He found employment in Stuarts Draft at H. K. Porter Company (the present Nibco) but lasted only two weeks before he realized that factory work was not for him. "It was hard being indoors with someone else telling you what to do all the time," laughed Butch. So he went back to logging for a few years, then in 1975, he applied for a job at Augusta Lumber in Staunton. He got the job, but at their Tennessee operation.

So the family moved to Tennessee where Butch began his career as a log scaler, buying paulownia trees—what the locals call "coffee wood"—for export purposes. After Butch bought the wood, it was taken to ports in New Orleans, Louisiana, and Savannah, Georgia, or it was brought back to Virginia.

Most of the lumber was shipped to Asian countries, Japan in particular. The Japanese made a traditional chest of drawers from Paulownia wood in which every woman kept her wedding dress and trousseau after marriage. Butch said he was fortunate enough in 1978 to have been able to visit several Japanese factories where the furniture was manufactured. He said paulownia wood was also used to make a musical instrument called a "koto," which was stringed and stood about six feet tall. Butch said it was very fascinating to visit a different country to see how they did things there. He recalls one factory that had a machine capable of slicing the paulownia into paper-thin strips that were then used as a veneer over other, less-desirable wood.

Butch explained the difference between the two kinds of pulp-wood: softwood and hardwood. Most softwood pulp is pine; it used for writing paper, milk cartons, and the like. Hardwoods are oak, gum, maple, and hickory; this pulp is ground up and used for making heavy cardboard.

I've always heard the older folks talk about extract wood, but I had never been sure exactly what it was. Butch explained that extract is dead-standing chestnut wood that is cut into five-foot lengths and sold; it is later chewed up and used for tanning leather. The H. D. Lee Company in Buena Vista is where most of the extract wood was taken to be sold. The company stopped buying extract in the late 1950s and later went out of business. Butch says with a sigh that back then, they were paid about thirteen dollars a cord for extract wood. "If we had it now, and we cut it for lumber, we'd be looking at a small fortune."

The Allen family moved back to Virginia in June 1980; Butch continued to work for Augusta Lumber until February 1981. It was at this time that he decided to ride out to Raphine and talk to

Calvert Fitzgerald of Fitzgerald Lumber Company about hiring him as a log scaler. Calvert told him to go back to Augusta Lumber, give his two-week notice, and stay quit for two weeks; then he'd hire him on. Butch was with Calvert until he retired.

Butch didn't require any equipment to do his job except a four-foot rule for measuring the length and diameter of a log. He says they bought logs eight- to sixteen-feet long with a minimum diameter of twelve inches, which is the normal measurement sawmills buy. When asked what a "big tree" in today's market would be, Butch says that a tree twenty-four inches on the small end would be considered big. He explains that they always measured from the small end of the tree because once the sawing begins, the little end gives you the face on the lumber. The excess is cut off and put in a chipper, producing by-products such as shavings, mulch, and sawdust, which is later sold.

Butch measuring a log at the Fitzgerald Lumber Company in Fairfield, Virginia

Part of Butch's job was to look at the logs when they came in to see if they were clear, which means how clean they are and whether they have any knots or imperfections in them. He could tell just by looking at a log how much money it would bring. He says that every Tuesday or Wednesday, they would get a market report from the Hardwood Association letting them know what price the different types of lumber were bringing. At the time of this interview, poplar logs were paying $550.00 a thousand (board feet), which means that a sixteen-foot clear poplar log with a twenty-inch diameter would have around 256 board feet in it, making it worth about $123.00. The average logger brings in one or two truckloads a day and can either get their check the same day or wait until they finish cutting for the week before being paid.

When asked what the most valuable wood was at that particular time, Butch said walnut was the top seller, then poplar. Most poplar is now exported to Italy. In years past, red oak was a top seller. And the beautiful paulownia? No longer in demand.

Butch is quick to say that now he's retired, he misses the people he had seen day in and day out over the years. The regulars who'd come to the sawmill each week with truckloads of logs, and the little guys who'd bring in from one to five logs in a pickup or on a trailer. Butch once said, "We buy from farmers who bring in one log that's fallen across a fence line, and they, in turn, buy more fence posts and lumber from us." He laughs and says the only thing he hadn't seen in twenty-eight years was someone roll in with a log in the trunk of a car!

He says people don't have to call when they want to bring a load of logs in, they just need to know what days and what hours the sawmill is buying. In years past, Fitzgerald Lumber bought Monday through Thursday from daylight until 4:30 p.m. and on Fridays from daylight until 3:30 p.m. Their policy now is Monday through Thursday, daylight until 4:30 p.m. but no Friday buying hours.

The current economy has affected some of the smaller loggers, forcing them out of business. The same goes for some sawmills, which are closing, too. Because the construction and housing market is down, not as much lumber is being sold today as in years past.

I asked Butch what he's going to do with all his spare time. He didn't take long to think about it—he's going spring mushroom hunting, will work in the garden, sleep late, and, come fall, go hunting every day of the season. You've earned it, Butch; enjoy your long vacation.

31

The Blue Ridge Parkway[*]

In September 1935, the solitude of the people who inhabited the Blue Ridge Mountains was broken. Isolated areas that were once cut off from mainstream society were laid open as a 1930s Depression make-work program was instituted. Most of the mountain people thought it was a joke. How could anyone begin to imagine a paved roadway that would stretch nearly five hundred miles along the crest of the Blue Ridge and connect with the Great Smoky Mountains in North Carolina? There were mixed feelings at best.

On one side of the coin, the mountain people did not want their land chopped in two, opening their farms up to outsiders' eyes. Up until this point, their lives had been extremely private and virtually free of strangers. There was only one road up the mountain, and everyone knew who came and went. Most were blood kin that had lived in the area for generations.

On the flip side, the men knew that this would at last be a sure-fire way to earn a good living for their families without having to leave the area. A secure government job was no farther than a step or two out the back door.

Some came willingly, eager for the chance to better their standard of living. Others were reluctant and fought bitterly to hold onto the rough but fertile land that had been in their families for

---

[*]Portions of this chapter came from information on Wikipedia.

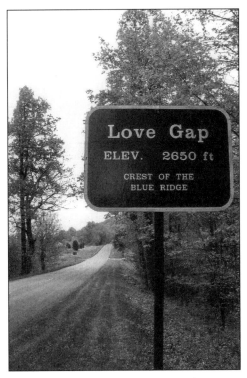

Love Gap on the Blue Ridge Parkway at milepost 16

generations. It was a hard decision for many to make, and there were more than a few fence sitters.

In the end, the project won out. Over the years, by a slow, piecemeal effort, tracts of land were purchased so that the Parkway could be completed. Our family was not spared; the Parkway acquired five acres of Coffey land bordering the roadway at Love Gap. From the beginning, the government instituted careful restrictions that ensured the future beauty and simplicity of the Blue Ridge Parkway, preserving the rural authenticity and quiet peace of the hills for generations to come.

The first time I traveled on the Parkway, looking at the fog-shrouded mountains, I felt a sense of awe. It looked as if someone had flung a blue-velvet cloak in the air, and it had landed in soft folds among the ridges. The log cabins and rustic wooden barns dotting the landscape took me back to an era when life was simpler. I never tire of looking out the windows of our own cabin to view the ancient hills surrounding us.

Actual construction of the Blue Ridge Parkway began in September 1935, on a twelve-and-a-half-mile section on the Virginia/North Carolina border. Most of the men employed were nearby residents, Civilian Conservation Corps workers, and conscientious objectors who would rather build than go to war. These hearty men did the actual labor on the road. Others necessary to the project were highway engineers, naturalists, landscape architects, blasting experts, and historians. There were also a number of European stonemasons brought in to teach others how to cut and lay rock for the walls and underpasses lining the Parkway.

Much of the early construction was painstakingly done by hand. The convenience of chainsaws and huge earth-moving equipment came much later in the project. Many of my neighbors here in Love who had worked on the construction said that they cleared trees with nothing more than crosscut saws and moved massive rocks with wooden levers. They all agreed that the ten-mile stretch from Humpback Rock to Love was one of the hardest sections. But their perseverance and backbreaking work paid big dividends for those of us who now enjoy the fruits of their labor. We have them to thank, along with the foresight of President Franklin D. Roosevelt, the Department of Interior, and the states of Virginia and North Carolina, for instituting the scenic roadway that winds its way through some of the most beautiful and unspoiled land this country has to offer.

Construction of the parkway took more than fifty-two years to complete; the last stretch of highway near the Linn Cove Viaduct was laid around Grandfather Mountain in 1987. There are twenty-six tunnels on the Blue Ridge Parkway, dug straight through the rock; one on the Virginia side and the other twenty-five in North Carolina. The highest point on the parkway, at 6,053 feet, is just south of Waynesville, near Mount Pisgah in North Carolina, on Richland Balsam Mountain at milepost 431. The road crosses streams, railway ravines, and other roads by way of 168 bridges and six viaducts. The Blue Ridge Parkway crosses the Virginia/North Carolina state line at mile 216.9. The 1749 party that surveyed the boundary included Peter Jefferson, father of Thomas Jefferson.

The parkway runs from the southern terminus of Shenandoah National Park's Skyline Drive in Waynesboro, Virginia, at Rockfish Gap and runs to U.S. Route 441 at Oconaluftee in the Great Smoky Mountains National Park near Cherokee, North Carolina. One of the most advantageous aspects for tourist travel is the fact that there is no fee for using the parkway; however, commercial vehicles are prohibited without prior approval from Park Service Headquarters near Asheville, North Carolina, and the speed limit is never higher than forty-five miles per hour.

The parkway uses short side roads to connect to highways. There are no direct interchanges with interstate highways, making it possible to enjoy wildlife and other scenery without having to stop for cross-traffic. Major towns and cities along the parkway include Waynesboro, Roanoke, and Galax in Virginia; in North Carolina, Boone and Asheville, where it runs across the property of the Biltmore Estate. The Blue Ridge Music Center, which is also part of the park, is located in Galax; Mount Mitchell, which is the highest point in eastern North America, is only accessible via a state road from the parkway at mile 355.4.

Wildflowers abound in the spring, including rhododendrons and dogwoods, moving from valleys to mountains as the cold weather retreats. Smaller annuals and perennials, such as daisies and asters, flower through the summer months. Brilliant autumn colors start in mid-September and continue through October, to the delight of those wishing to take memorable photographs.

Major trees include oak, hickory, and the tulip tree at lower elevations, buckeye and ash in the middle, and conifers such as fir and spruce at the highest elevations. Often, the trees near the higher peaks and ridges take on distorted shapes because of the high winds and persistent rime ice in the winter.

The slower speeds on the parkway afford a close-up view of the many types of animals that inhabit the forestlands. Bears, fox, deer, raccoons, and bobcats have all been spotted by locals and tourists alike.

There are a number of stopping-off places along the parkway that are well worth the visit. For a complete list, just go to www.BlueRidgeParkway.org or contact your closest National Park office.

In September 2010, the Blue Ridge Parkway will celebrate its seventy-fifth anniversary with many events being planned for throughout the year. No other scenic roadway attracts as many visitors from the U.S. and abroad. In 2006, I worked as a seasonal interpretive ranger at the Humpback Rocks pioneer farm; I was amazed at how many visitors we had from France, Holland, Germany, Africa, Italy, and many other countries. All were very interested in the Appalachian culture and were surprised to learn that they could enjoy the variety of interpretive sites without charge.

We salute the great American treasure known as the Blue Ridge Parkway. May your beauty and character always stand firm for the future, so that our children and grandchildren can witness the hidden joys of rural mountain life that lie along each bend in your winding road. From Rockfish Gap, Virginia, to the entrance of the Great Smoky Mountains in North Carolina—happy anniversary!

Cabin at the Humpback Rocks Pioneer Farm at milepost 5.8

Evergreen Christian Church, Nash, Virginia

Backroads

Lyle Bradley; Vesuvius, Virginia

Where do all the backroads end
and where do they start?
They are roadways that lead us
to places so dear to our hearts.

A log cabin in some deep hollow
or an old homestead on a hill;
Places with names that ring so true
Love, Piney River, Montebello, Massies Mill.

There's Coffeytown and Vesuvius,
Fork Mountain and Crabtree Falls;
Irish Creek and the Forks of Buffalo
and many places I can't recall.

There's Cornwall down in Rockbridge
and Lovingston, the Nelson County seat;
The dark red mud of Amherst
that's so hard to get off your feet.

The North and South Fork of Tye River
and Old Pedlar that runs so clear;
And the five big drops on the Crabtree
many people dreadfully fear.

Shoe Creek is filled with native trout
as down the mountain she flows;
And a hemlock hollow behind Spy Rock
where a patch of ginseng still grows.

They all can be reached by backroads
and they're not too hard to find;
I visit them all many times each year
if only in my mind.

About the Author

Even as a child, Lynn Coffey had a Waldenish bent toward a nineteenth-century existence, despite the fact that she was growing up along the busy Gold Coast of southern Florida, with all the amenities of modern living. Her dream was to someday live in a log cabin in the mountains and live a quiet, self-sufficient lifestyle.

Lynn began living that dream upon moving to the tiny hamlet of Love, Virginia, in the summer of 1980. As she met and got to know her neighbors, all of whom were quite elderly at the time, she soon realized the culture of these hearty Scottish/Irish descendants was slowly vanishing and needed to be preserved.

Without any formal education or prior experience in journalism, Lynn carved out a folksy niche of documenting early Appalachian life through the pages of a monthly newspaper called *Backroads*, the first issue being published in December 1981. For the next twenty-five years, *Backroads* chronicled the history of the mountain people as Lynn traveled the hills and hollers, interviewing the elders and photographing handicrafts and activities that had been handed down for generations.

In the process, little did she realize how entwined their lives would become or how much the mountain people would come to mean to her as they opened their hearts to trust a young woman who started out as an "outsider" and ended up becoming one of them.

You can request additional copies of *Backroads* by using this order form.

ORDER FORM

Name _____

Address _____

City, State, Zip _____

Please send me _____ copies of *Backroads* at $20.00 each plus $5.00 per book shipping.

Make checks or money orders payable to Lynn Coffey and mail to:

Lynn Coffey
1461 Love Road
Lyndhurst, VA 22952